THE
RISHA LEVINSON
STORY

RISHA W. LEVINSON

THE
RISHA LEVINSON
STORY

GROWING UP IN THE
GREATEST GENERATION

with

MARTIN H. LEVINSON

iUniverse, Inc.
Bloomington

The Risha Levinson Story
Growing Up in the Greatest Generation

iUniverse books may be ordered through booksellers or by contacting:

iUniverse
1663 Liberty Drive
Bloomington, IN 47403
www.iuniverse.com
1-800-Authors (1-800-288-4677)

ISBN: 978-1-4759-7648-9 (sc)
ISBN: 978-1-4759-7649-6 (ebk)

Printed in the United States of America

iUniverse rev. date: 03/06/2013

For my family and faith

The Greatest Generation is a term coined by journalist Tom Brokaw to describe the generation that grew up in the United States during the hard times of the Great Depression and then went on to fight in World War II, as well as those whose productivity on the war's home front made a material contribution to the war effort. The generation is sometimes referred to as the *G.I. Generation,* an expression coined by historians William Strauss and Neil Howe.

Contents

Chapter 1

The Early Years in Milwaukee

I was born on September 23, 1920, in Milwaukee, Wisconsin. My sister Sarah was also born in Milwaukee, seventeen months earlier. My brother Joe, who is seven years older than me, was born in Russia and brought to the US, via Japan, by my mother, Dora (Yiddish name Dubba). They were supposed to have gone to Columbus, Wisconsin but went first instead to Columbus, Ohio because my mother asked the railroad ticket agent in San Francisco for a ticket to Columbus but did not specify the state.

Dad (English name Harry, Yiddish name Aaron) came from the Russian Empire to America, which was regarded by the Jewish community in Russia as *die goldene medina* (Yiddish for the golden land), before Mom in 1913. Wrapping a handkerchief around his jaw so as to appear, face hidden, a toothache victim, he escaped the Tsar's army, journeying by train across the Empire's border to Poland. After suffering through two nights in the border forest between Poland and Germany, he made his way to the port city of Hamburg, Germany. From there he took a steamship to Quebec, Canada and then traveled to Wisconsin, where his sister and brother-in-law were living, to make a new life for himself and his family.

Dad had married Mom back in the old country in 1911. She was a twenty-one-year-old seamstress. He was a nineteen-year-old hat-maker's apprentice. When he was eighteen, he had gone to my mother's town, Kalenkovich, near the Polish-Russian border, to escape the draft. My mother's family took him in and my mother's father, Meyer Pickman, who was known in the village as Meyer *der kirzhner* (the hat maker), taught Harry the hat-making trade.

One day Meyer discovered Harry and Dubba walking hand in hand and declared them engaged on the spot. They were married shortly thereafter in a home ceremony and soon after that, within the first year of their marriage, my brother Joe was born.

With the assistance of his *mishpocha* (relatives) Dad made his way to Fort Atkinson, Wisconsin, to try to get a business started and make enough money so he could settle down. Several years later, in Columbus, Wisconsin, he began to make the transition from itinerant peddler of scrap metal to chicken feed supplier to cattle butchering.

In 1917, he wrote to his wife to join him. Unable to go through Western Europe because of World War I battles being waged there, my mother went east with Joe from Kiev to Vladivostok, a distance of over 4,400 miles, on the Trans-Siberian Railroad, the longest train ride in the world. They then took a boat to Yokohama, Japan, and after six weeks in that city boarded a steamship for San Francisco, finally arriving in the United States sometime in late 1917 or early 1918. (My son Daniel uncovered much of the foregoing information and shared it with guests who came to celebrate my ninetieth birthday party in 2010.)

Business wasn't so good for Dad in Columbus and when an occasion arose for him to open a butcher shop in Milwaukee he took it, moving our family to a four-story brick building in a working-class Jewish neighborhood on the corner of Fourteenth and Galena Street. Our family lived on the second and third floors of that structure: the second floor contained a kitchen, a pantry, a dining room with a large round oak table, a walnut carved buffet, and a Victrola record player; the third floor contained our sleeping quarters. The fourth floor of the building had several bedrooms that were occupied by boarders. The first floor was Dad's butcher shop.

Milwaukee was a magnet for foreign immigrants in the nineteenth and early-twentieth centuries. In the 1850s, many German Jews, escaping from the anti-Semitic proclivities of Imperial Germany, arrived in Milwaukee and later lots of Eastern European Jews, escaping from the anti-Semitic inclinations of Imperial Russia, streamed in. By 1910, Milwaukee shared the distinction with New York City of having the largest proportion of foreign-born residents in the United States.

The basement of our Milwaukee home housed laundry equipment that included huge cylindrical washtubs and a large scrub board over which Mom spent many hours rubbing and scrubbing so long and so hard that she developed tender raw blisters between her fingers. Other laundry items included bleach, starch, and bluing that needed to be prepared with hot water. Clothes for steam ironing were wrapped up in terrycloth towels to retain moisture, and laundry starch was added to produce a smooth, stiff finish when the starched material was ironed.

I loved feeling the steam vapor that came up from the boiling hot water in the basement washtubs. One day, while playing, Sarah carried me over one of the steaming tubs. Thoughtlessly, I lowered one foot into that scorching cauldron and received a terrible burn. Fortunately, Mom dashed to my rescue. She snatched me from Sarah, dressed the burn with Mazola oil, covered the wound with baking soda, and applied layers of gauze to my injured appendage. I wept uncontrollably through the entire procedure.

When I was five, I gave Mom more trouble by falling out of our second floor window on the Fourth of July. As it was a very warm day, I had decided to climb up and sit on the screened windowsill. Not a good move! When I leaned against the screen it gave way and I fell, along with the screen, to the cement sidewalk below. Luckily, the screen acted as a buffer and I was fortuitously saved from serious injury. Dad, who was shaving at the time and saw me plummet past the bathroom window, ran down the stairs, picked me up, and carried me into the house. I vaguely recall a cluster of neighbors and passersby in the dining room as Mom, tears cascading down her face, cradled me in her arms. The only other time I remember my mother crying so hard was when Sarah had to be taken to the hospital for a mastoid operation.

Regarding operations, the same year I dropped from the window I had an appendectomy, which resulted in a ten-day stay at Mt. Sinai Hospital. Mom visited me each day I was there. Poor Mom. She would hold my hand and sleep during her visits, apparently out of sheer exhaustion. Riding the trolley car was stressful for Mom, given her limited eyesight and self-consciousness about making herself understood in English. She was also depleted from hand-washing all the family laundry, shopping for everybody (a difficult task for her because she had "milk leg," a chronic condition of deep vein thrombosis that she acquired during her pregnancies), climbing the stairs with young children, preparing canned foods and meals for our family and for neighbors from the old country who stopped by, and sewing everyone's clothes. Mom battled her fatigue daily until she died at the age of fifty-one, worn to a frazzle from her countless responsibilities.

One of those responsibilities was arranging for *Pesach* (the Hebrew word for the festival of *Passover*), which involved (a) helping Dad make wine; (b) preparing sour pickles, canned fruits, and the rest of the Pesach meal; (c) thoroughly cleaning the entire house, washing every window, and putting up fresh draperies and; (d) a whole bunch more. I got to hate Passover and cried myself to sleep at night because I worried that Mom would never make it through the holiday. Just like the Jews were enslaved to Pharaoh in the land of Egypt, Mom was a slave to a celebration commemorating Jewish freedom in the land of beer and cheese.

(NB: Passover is the Jewish holiday of the feast of unleavened bread [*matzo*]. It commemorates the story of the Exodus, in which the ancient Israelites were freed from slavery in Egypt. One of the most widely observed Jewish holidays, Passover begins on the fifteenth day of the month of Nisan in the Jewish calendar and is celebrated for seven or eight days.)

My brother Joe delivered the *Milwaukee Journal* every morning riding on his bicycle. That's a job I would never have been allowed to do because it was considered *es past nit* (unbecoming) for young girls in my social circle to ride bikes. Joe was a hard-working paperboy and a good student. In his spare time he read westerns and Horatio Alger stories. The latter were formulaic rags-to-riches tales in which young men, by leading exemplary lives and struggling valiantly against poverty and adversity, gain both wealth and honor, ultimately realizing the American Dream. Alger's yarns were quite popular among adolescent males in the 1920s.

Joe loved playing with his dog Brownie, a mutt he adopted that was not permitted in the house. After finishing his paper route Joe would feed Brownie and then have a savory breakfast of donuts and tea for himself. Mom and Dad referred to their brood as "Joseph and the *meydls*" (young girls).

The social life of the family centered around the *landsleit*, kinfolk who had migrated from their little *shtetls* (small towns) in the Pale of Settlement, a term given to an area within Imperial Russia in which permanent settlement of Jews was allowed, and beyond which Jewish residency was generally prohibited. Mom's little shtetl was Kalenkovich; Dad was brought up in Skarodne. Both towns were located at the southern or Ukrainian end of the Pale.

The Pale of Settlement encompassed about twenty percent of the territory of European Russia, and included much of present-day Lithuania, Belarus, Poland, Moldova, Ukraine, and parts of western Russia. Living conditions were not easy for Jews in the Pale, a region that was like a huge reservation similar to those in the western United States where Native Americans were forced to live in the late 1800s. The problems of Jewish life in the Pale have been portrayed by a number of nineteenth-century Yiddish authors, the most celebrated being Sholom Aleichem, whose stories of Tevye the Milkman in the fictional shtetl of Anatevka comprise the core of *Fiddler on the Roof.*

In 1881, Russia began evicting Jews from the Pale of Settlement, which began as a mass migration. By 1914, two million Jews had left the Pale and settled in Germany, Austria, America, and other countries. The Pale of Settlement lasted until 1917, when it was abolished by the Russian Provisional Government.

Associations with village life remained precious to many of the new immigrants from the Russian Empire, who bonded with each other over such connections by forming *landsmanschaften*—societies made up people from the same hometown or local region who felt their close ties of origin gave them a special affinity not only for friendship but for mutual aid and encouragement. My parents were part of a *landsmanschaft* in Milwaukee that called itself the *Kalenkovich Skarodner Untershtitsung Farayn* (the Kalenkovich Skarodne Benevolent Society).

On weekends, our family often visited fellow *landsmen* (Jewish compatriots from the same area of origin). I particularly liked dropping in on the Kamesars, a wealthy landsleit family that lived in a large and attractive home on Sherman Boulevard. I envied their house but more than that I coveted the amazing collection of toys the Kamesar children had, especially their posh dolls and baby strollers. My parents could not afford to buy expensive dolls and baby strollers for my sister and me but I did have one special plaything: a little red-cloth dog with a zippered pocket that came with my little red winter coat. I absolutely adored that burgundy-colored canine, which served me as both toy and surrogate pet.

Kopel and Chanah, a happy-go-lucky landsleit couple, resided in a spacious, well-furnished house in a nondescript part of town. They seemed to enjoy life, especially at the *simkhes* (parties) that they hosted. Kopel was loud and boisterous at these affairs and, not being shy, I imitated Kopel—stomping, shouting, and being somewhat rowdy—while his guests cheered me on and gleefully howled at my antics. But what really gave me a thrill was emulating Dad's elegant mode of Chassidic dancing at these get-togethers and at other family meetings.

Dad was a handsome, debonair fellow who used a cigarette holder when he smoked and a smooth line of patter when he flirted with women. People extolled his urbane outlook and cheerful personality at landsleit revelries. They also praised his imaginative Chassidic dances in which I frequently joined him, copying and elaborating on his graceful choreography.

Our father daughter dancing duo typically attracted lots of attention, which was not always easy for or acceptable to my sister Sarah, who did not have my drive and *chutzpah* (supreme self-confidence) to act like a "Jewish ham." However, Sarah's charm, beauty, and stately grace gained her notice of her own.

I liked listening to the records that were played on our upright mahogany Victrola, particularly the liturgical recordings of Cantor Pierre Pinchik, one of the cantorial giants of America's golden age of *Hazzanut* (the Hebrew word for cantor is *hazzan*). I also liked hearing *Oh Promise Me,* a song from a "light opera" that with its beautiful melody and wonderful sentiment is still sung at weddings. The only classical record I recall listening to on our Victrola was George Enescu's *Romanian Rhapsody,* a musical piece that features vivid Romanian rhythms and an air of spontaneity.

As Sarah and I grew older it was expected that we would learn to play the piano. And so Mom and Dad purchased an Estey Baby Grand, which took up most of the space in our living room. The Estey was a symbol of culture and refinement that my parents hoped would motivate my sister and me to acquire an appreciation for the fine arts. Such an understanding was considered essential for middle-class Jewish girls growing up in Milwaukee.

While our Baby Grand was regal and elegant, Mrs. Hammer, our piano teacher, possessed neither of those attributes. She was instead rather nervous and uninspiring. But we went along with our lessons anyway and even played duets in public for which we were ill prepared and therefore not very good. After two years of instruction, Mrs. Hammer passed away and, truth be told, Sarah and I really didn't feel all that bad that she was no longer among the living.

When I was sixteen, I resumed piano lessons with a talented young pianist by the name of Beatrice Sharp, who performed in public as Bea Sharp—an appellation that brings to mind the musical note C natural. Sadly, I wasn't able to take piano lessons on a regular basis due to the busy schedules that Bea and I both had. However, I relished my piano instruction and vowed to continue to take lessons and play music someday as an adult, a promise I eventually honored, taking up the violin in my late thirties and becoming proficient enough on it that I played first violin with the Adelphi University Symphony Orchestra for a number of years.

The Nelsons, who lived across the street from us, were our neighborhood grocers. They were hard-working people who operated their small provisions store from dawn to midnight. Mom regarded the Nelsons as models of parental success, as their two children were highly educated teachers who played piano. Mom wanted her progeny to be just like the Nelson offspring—scholarly and accomplished.

The Hootkins were my favorite grocers, especially the lovable and plump Mrs. Hootkin, who helped her sick husband manage an unassuming grocery market located crosswise from my elementary school. Their store carried a wide assortment of penny candies and even nickel candies—for the rich kids. I fantasized about sampling all the goodies that the Hootkins set out in an old glass mahogany display case: the licorice whips, the chocolate-covered peppermint wafers, the sour balls, the Fralinger's Salt Water Taffy, the diminutive round colored candy dots that had to be picked off the paper they adhered to. Regrettably, I had but one stomach and a limited supply of funds for sweets.

Mrs. Hootkin always gave me extra candies with my two-cent purchase. She was a very sweet lady who genuinely loved children, greeting them with great giant hugs and kisses on the cheek when they came through the door. I particularly admired the Hootkins for the loving acceptance they gave their visibly retarded son. He was barely able to communicate but was given liberty to roam the streets at will where he was warmly received by neighbors and even strangers.

I also revered my father, a smart and savvy businessman with a *Yiddeshe kop* (a Yiddish expression for someone who is on the ball). Though he couldn't read or write English, Dad was capable of signing his name and astute in reading stock market quotes in the daily newspaper. That combination, and a natural instinct for making good business deals, helped him to make a pretty penny through investing in equities.

When I was six, Dad sold his butcher shop to Abe, a landsman who occupied one of the apartments in our building. With the proceeds from the sale he opened a wholesale meat delivery business and then a kosher slaughterhouse named United Dressed Beef that he ran during World War II.

Dad drove about in an open truck to make his meat deliveries. That vehicle also served as our family car and occasionally we took family excursions in it to places like the shores of Lake Michigan, where we had barrels of fun swimming, picnicking, and taking long walks on the beach. On some of our trips Sarah and I would sit in the back of the truck and sing songs and flirt with drivers on the road. Our favorite song to sing to those motorists was "Oh, you nasty man."

Our iceman, the fellow who filled up the family icebox with blocks of ice, was the emphatic opposite of a nasty man. He was a gent who did an extremely arduous and straining job, which began at around four o'clock in the morning each day and lasted until he finished late in the evening. If you didn't want your food to spoil it was very important to make sure your icebox had enough ice in it, a concern that was especially crucial in the summer. Nowadays, people take refrigeration for granted. Not me. I know what a boon it is *to not* wait to have the iceman cometh.

After Dad sold his butcher shop to Abe, our family moved to a detached two-story house on a steep hill on Forty-Sixth Street. The hill was an enormous hardship for Mom, as her milk-leg condition made walking difficult even on flat surfaces. There was also a large garbage dump in back of the house that nobody in our family cared for. However, the neighborhood was considered a lot better than the one we had moved from, so we all tried to take the negatives in stride.

Sarah and I were able to ride the trolley cars that were only two blocks from where we lived. But Mom didn't like taking the trolley. She worried people might try to talk to her in English and she wouldn't understand them. So she schlepped on foot to do shopping and other essential errands for the family.

Dad tried to make life more comfortable for Mom by hiring domestic workers to help her with the housework. But his wife would have none of that. Mom simply redoubled her efforts and wound up working twice as hard as the domestics did. We ultimately moved to a bigger house on Fifty-Second Street in a much fancier part of town. To quote a familiar song lyric, we were "movin' on up."

Relatives

The only relations we had in Milwaukee were Dad's older sister Rebecca (Tante Rivka), a hypochondriac aunt who constantly *kvetched* (complained) about her various aches and pains, and her husband Joe (Onkel Joe Free), who totally worshiped his petulant wife.

The Frees lived in a chic apartment in a swanky quarter of the city. They were unable to have children of their own so they adopted Rivka's nephew Ben, following his bar mitzvah in Chicago. Ben's mother, Chaya Sora, had died of typhoid in Russia and left a family of eight children. Her husband Israel agreed to

Ben's adoption, since raising eight kids without a spouse was an immense burden for him.

Sarah and I adored cousin Ben, who was very handsome, gentle, and kind. Sarah liked Ben so much she wanted to marry him, but he was not ready to walk down the aisle at the time of her infatuation. Ben later became an attorney.

Tante Rivka and Onkel Joe were the only couple I knew who showed outward affection for each other. I never saw my mother and father behave romantically. In fact, years later I realized Dad had never given Mom a wedding band and she had never asked for one. Concern over their children is what bound my parents together, with Dad being responsible to get the money to keep the family going and Mom being responsible to carefully manage it. Besides having Tante Rivka and Onkel Joe as romantic role models, Sarah and I learned about romance through movies, popular magazines, and novels.

Mom had a tough time being around Tante Rivka because Rivka would remind her that she had the advantage of being literate in both English and Yiddish, which enabled Rivka to be elected president of the David Pinsky Women's Club, a Labor Zionist organization that Mom belonged to as well. Rivka was also a member of the Farband (the Jewish National Workers Alliance), Pioneer Women of America, Hadassah, ORT (the Society for Trades and Agricultural Labor), the Ladies Auxiliary of Congregation Beth Israel, the Milwaukee Jewish Home for the Aged, Mount Sinai Hospital Ladies Auxiliary, Milwaukee Hebrew Sheltering Home, Milwaukee Jewish Convalescent Home, Milwaukee Jewish Children's Home, Beth Am Center, and the Order of the Eastern Star.

Rivka's tendency for self-praise and her boasting about the accolades she received from her fellow club members about the homespun poetry she wrote were difficult for Mom to tolerate, particularly since Mom was never able to find the time or opportunity to complete her part-time English classes at the local high school. But Mom took comfort in being an excellent parent to her children, a feat that no other achievement could possibly match.

Dad's younger brother, Yanke Moshe, was a cantor who lived in Chicago; a city situated ninety miles from Milwaukee. Occasionally we would visit Yanke Moshe, who was weighed down with a family of five sickly children, most likely the result of the close blood relation between mother and father—Yanke Moshe's wife, Minnie, had been his niece. Four of his children died before becoming adults. The fifth, a redheaded trumpet player named Max, survived and went on to have a very successful career playing music with his wife, who was also a musician.

Chapter 2

A Young Girl's Education

Elementary School

My first four years at Neeskara Public School were easy and fun, more so after I mastered the *Red Rover* primers, the 1920s version of *Dick and Jane,* which I literally memorized. I was the teacher's pet in Mrs. Ziller's fourth grade class, a role I genuinely loved and entirely got into. When Mrs. Ziller asked me to remain at recess to file her nails and puff-out the erasers it was like I was in heaven. But my happiness with school was short-circuited when I was promoted, due to good grades, in the middle of the school year from class 4A to 5A.

In Mrs. Conway's fifth-grade class I was no longer the star pupil. And to make matters worse, I had a difficult time with fractions, which dealt a serious blow to the image I had of myself as a *chochem* (a genius). One thing that helped make those awful conditions tolerable was coming home for lunch each day to feast on Mom's homemade victuals: fare like pickled herring in a large glass bowl, chicken soup with *lokshen* (noodles), crab apples, *gefilte* fish (a Jewish dish made from a poached mixture of ground deboned fish, such as carp, whitefish and/or pike), *borscht* (beet soup), fresh baked bread, and delicious preserves bottled in Mason jars.

I also found solace in going with Sarah to the movies, which frequently featured Westerns where we booed the villains and cheered the heroes—fellows like Hollywood's first Western megastar, Tom Mix, the "king of the cowboys." All Westerns contained the same basic elements: the valiant cowboy wiped out all traces of evil from a frontier town and then won the girl in the end. Call me a square, but that formula worked flawlessly for me.

Jews and Motion Pictures

Neil Gabler, in his compelling and well-researched book *An Empire of Their Own* (1989), describes how the Jews invented Hollywood. He notes that Jewish immigrants, or children of immigrants, were the founding fathers of nearly every major Hollywood studio. These individuals, men such as Harry Warner of Warner Brothers (born in Poland), Carl Laemmle of Universal Pictures (born in Germany), Adolph Zukor of Paramount Pictures (born in Hungary), William Fox of Fox Film Corporation (born in Hungary), Louis B. Mayer of MGM (born in Russia), and Harry Cohn of Columbia Pictures (born in New York City to Russian-German-Jewish parents) ran almost all the big movie studios in the 1930s where they produced and mass-marketed their vision of the American Dream.

Here are some other historical tidbits concerning Jews and the movies: The first American feature film, *The Great Train Robbery* (1912) featured a Jew, Gilbert M. "Broncho Billy" Anderson, in the lead; the first large Hollywood production, from Adolph Zukor's Paramount, was *Queen Elizabeth* (1912), starring the unparalleled stage and film actress Sarah Bernhardt, *aka* "The Divine Sarah"; the first full-length nationally distributed talking film, *The Jazz Singer* (1927), the story of a young man who rejects the wish of his father, a cantor, to become a cantor, spotlighted Al Jolson (birth name: Asa Yoelson), a Russian-Jewish émigré who in his heyday was dubbed "The World's Greatest Entertainer." *The Jazz Singer* was really the story of Jolson's life.

The Yiddish Folk Shule and Labor Zionism

Learning the *aleph-bet* (ABCs) at the Yiddish folk *shule* (school) was a sheer delight for me, as Mom and Dad were Yiddish-speaking and I could share my newfound knowledge with them. I also enjoyed socializing with the kids at the folk shule, where we were all inspired by the Labor Zionist movement, a cause that advocated founding the Jewish national home on Jewish labor. My years of attendance at the folk shule, which began when I was eight, sparked what would become a lifelong interest for me in Yiddish and Zionism. That included having people call me by my Yiddish name Risha, a designation I have used all my adult life rather than my given name Rose.

(A Pokemyname.com note on the name *Risha*: Risha is the 20,924[th] most popular name in the USA. One in every 351,102 Americans is named Risha and the popularity of the name Risha is 2.85 people per million. It is estimated, as of February 28, 2012, that there are 894 people named Risha in the United States and the number is increasing by seven every year.)

The Yiddish folk shule in Milwaukee was one of many Jewish folk institutes in America that had as their purpose to acquaint American Jewish youth with their Jewish historical and cultural past and to instill in them a desire to perpetuate Jewish culture. Its goal was to be a place of joy, where children would be stimulated by ideas and learning. The folk shule's wide-ranging curriculum included:

- Yiddish—Reading, writing, conversation, grammar, and literature
- Hebrew—Reading, writing, conversation, grammar, and literature
- History—Jewish legends and history from its earliest periods to the present day
- Hebrew Bible Study—Selections from the greatest story ever told
- Jewish Music—Folk songs, national songs, Jewish melodies, and songs of ancient and modern Palestine
- Jewish Folklore—Folk tales, anecdotes, etc.
- Jewish Holidays—Their meaning, observation, and celebration
- Talks—On daily topics, from Jewish life all over, especially in Palestine

Golda Meir (an Israeli teacher, kibbutznik, and politician who became the fourth Prime Minister of Israel) was a Yiddish folk shule teacher and a Labor Zionist. She and her family had come to the United States from Russia in 1906 to escape *pogroms*—mob attacks against Jews, characterized by killings and destruction of homes, businesses, and synagogues.

Notorious pogroms in the Russian Empire include the Odessa pogroms (1821, 1859, 1871, 1881-1906), Warsaw pogrom (1881), Kishinev pogrom (1903), Bialystok pogrom (1906), Lwów pogrom (1918), and Kiev pogroms (1919). Pogroms were for Russia what the circuses had been for ancient Rome—an outlet for the frustrations of the peasants who otherwise might have directed their terrible wrath against the rulers.

The Meirs wound up residing in a two-story flat in an impoverished Jewish neighborhood in Milwaukee. The area where they settled was so poor that their apartment had no electricity or bathroom. Living without those amenities could not have been very pleasant for Golda, but on the upside she didn't have to hide under her bed and worry about being beaten, raped, or killed by a bunch of crazy Cossacks in a pogrom.

Golda Meir's interest in public service was evident even when she was a girl. In the fourth grade, concerned that her classmates were too poor to buy schoolbooks, she organized the American Young Sisters Society to raise money to pay for them. When Golda began school she did not know English, but she graduated as the valedictorian of her class. Meir's early life in Milwaukee is described in greater detail in her riveting autobiography *My Life* (1975), which tells the story of a fantastically gifted woman who went from a poverty-stricken childhood in Kiev, Russia, to become a major player on the world's stage as Prime Minister of the State of Israel, a post she held from 1969 to 1974.

In 1917, Golda took a position at the folk shule where she came more closely into contact with the ideals of Labor Zionism. Four years later she left Milwaukee with her husband, Morris Meyerson, to join a *kibbutz* (a collective community that was traditionally based on agriculture and had as its goal "to make the dessert bloom") in Palestine. In 1928, she was elected secretary of *Moetzet HaPoalot* (Working Women's Council), which required her to spend two years (1932–34) as a Zionist emissary in the US promoting Labor Zionism.

Meir and her fellow Labor Zionists believed that to have a Jewish state, more needed to done than just asking powerful entities such as Britain, Germany, or the Ottoman Empire for their permission to have one. Rather, they thought a Jewish state could only be created through the efforts of the Jewish working class settling in Palestine and constructing a nation through the formation of a progressive Jewish society with rural kibbutzim and urban Jewish workers. David Ben-Gurion, the main founder and first Prime Minister of Israel, was a Labor Zionist.

During her term doing emissary work in America, Golda gave a lecture in Yiddish to a group of ladies at a meeting of the David Pinsky Women's Club in my parents' house. (I stayed home from school and helped Mom prepare cookies and cake for the occasion.) A few years later, in 1936, Mom met Golda Meir in the Holy Land and had her picture taken with the future prime minister of Israel—a woman who in her time would be as much esteemed as Queen Elizabeth and as well known by her first name as Madonna. Mom and Dad were able to make their trip to Palestine because of a money settlement Mom received from the Boston Store for an injury she incurred from a faulty entrance door to that retail outlet.

Mom gave me the photo of her and Golda Meir when I went to graduate school, and wherever I have lived in my life I have displayed it. Mom utterly and completely venerated Mrs. Meir. In my growing-up years she continuously told me she wanted me to be just like Golda.

At the folk shule I read Yiddish translations of the Bible on *Shabbat* (the seventh day of the Jewish week and the Jewish day of rest) and participated in special holiday programs. I rehearsed for these events with Mom, who was a wise and compassionate critic. I distinctly remember one Friday night recitation when I was preparing to read a poem by the Spanish Jewish physician, poet, and philosopher Yehuda Halevi. The subject was the yearning of Halevi to return to the Promised Land, and I was reciting his words to my mother with far too much fervor. She told me to slow down, smile when the text permits, vary your voice. That advice worked really well and my reading was a huge hit.

I was not the best-behaved child at the Yiddish folk shule. Chaver Melrood, my Yiddish teacher, went so far as to call my father to say to him "Please tell Risha to stop talking so much in class. She's a real *nudnik* (a bothersome person) and a disturbance to the other students." Mr. Kniaz, my music teacher, also reprimanded me from time to time for being a *nudje* (a pest) and talking out of turn in class. But beneath my fooling around I was seriously determined to become a Yiddish teacher—later a Yiddish-Hebrew teacher—and I never lost sight of that goal.

(NB: Yiddish is a High German language of Ashkenazi Jewish origin, spoken throughout the world. It developed as a fusion of German dialects with Hebrew, Aramaic, Slavic languages and traces of Romance languages. It is written in the Hebrew alphabet. Celebrated Yiddish writers include Sholem Aleichem, Mendele Mocher Sforim, Isaac Leib Peretz, and Isaac Bashevis Singer who won the Nobel Prize for Literature in 1978 "for his impassioned narrative art, which, with roots in a Polish-Jewish cultural tradition, bring universal human conditions to life." The word "Yiddish" is the Yiddish word for "Jewish," so it is technically correct to refer to the Yiddish language as "Jewish." It is never correct to refer to Hebrew as "Jewish.")

Because I knew Yiddish, I was able to read the *Forverts* (commonly known as the *Jewish Daily Forward)* newspaper to my mother, whose eyesight made it difficult for her to read it herself. Mom liked the recipes that were printed in the *Forward*, such as ones for meat *kreplach* (dumplings), *kugel* (baked pudding or casserole made from egg noodles or potatoes), *latkes* (potato pancakes), *matzo ball soup, kasha varnishkes* (buckwheat groats with bow tie noodles), and *babka* (a sweet yeasty cake). But her favorite part of the paper was the *Bintel Brief* (Yiddish for bundle of letters), an advice column for new Jewish immigrants to assist them with their new lives. The *Bintel Brief* was my preferred part of the paper too, and reading it every week to Mom was useful preparation for my eventual career as a social worker.

The following is a sample of actual *Bintel Brief* letters and answers. Examining them gives one a feel for why this section of the *Forward* was so interesting and relevant to new Jewish-American settlers. More missives and responses can be

17

found in Isaac Metzker's delightful book *A Bintel Brief: Sixty Years of Letters from the Lower East Side to the Jewish Daily Forward* (1990).

> *My dearest friends of the Forward,*
> I have been jobless for six months now. I have eaten the last shirt on my back and now there is nothing left for me but to end my life . . .
> *Answer*: This is one of hundreds of heartrending pleas for help, cries of need that we receive daily. The writer of this letter should go first to the Crisis Conference [address given], and they will not let him starve. And further we ask our readers to let us know if someone can create a job for this unemployed man.

> *Dear Editor,*
> I am a girl from Galicia [in Poland] and in the shop where I work I sit near a Russian Jew . . . he stated that all Galicians were no good . . . Why should one worker resent another?
> *Answer*: The Galician Jews are just as good and bad as people from other lands. If the Galicians must be ashamed of the foolish and evil ones among them, then the Russians too, must hide their heads in shame because among them there is such an idiot as the acquaintance of our letter writer.

> *Dear Editor,*
> For a long time I worked in a shop with a Gentile girl . . . and fell in love. But after we had been married for a year . . . I began to notice that whenever one of my Jewish friends came to the house, she was displeased.
> *Answer*: Unfortunately, we often hear of such tragedies, which stem from marriages between people of different worlds. It's possible that if this couple were to move to a Jewish neighborhood, the young man might have more influence on his wife.

The *Forward* began publishing in 1897 as a Yiddish-language daily put out by dissidents from the Socialist Labor Party. It was an important and tremendously inspiring read for people like my mother who were interested in all things Jewish. During the first three decades of the twentieth century the *Forward* achieved huge circulation and considerable political influence that spanned the world. It still exists in parallel Yiddish and English editions, and I'm delighted to report that the *Forward* has recently introduced a rejuvenated and enhanced Yiddish Web site complete with blogs and links to Facebook. I have a subscription to the *Yiddish Forward*, which I take great pleasure in reading.

A large part of my social life took place at the folk shule. Hinde, my best girl friend, was a folk shule chum as was Gittel, another gal pal. Both were part of a group of girls I associated with to share confidences, get support, and learn about sex and marriage. Hinde eventually made *aliyah*, a Hebrew term denoting ascent and the immigration of Jews to the land of Israel (emigration from Israel is referred to as *yerida* ["descent"]).

Making aliyah, a basic tenet of Zionism, is enshrined in the State of Israel's Law of Return—legislation that accords any Jew the legal right to assisted immigration and settlement in Israel, as well as Israeli citizenship. Going back to *Eretz Yisrael* has been a Jewish aspiration since the Babylonian exile. Large-scale immigration to the land of Israel started in the late nineteenth century. Since the birth of the State of Israel in 1948, two-and-a-half-million Jews from around the globe have made aliyah.

I had my first romantic relationship at the Yiddish folk shule. The object of my affections was a boy named Paul Melrood, the son of Chaver Melrood. Paul (*aka* "Pinkie," short for Pinchas) was an affable, handsome young man who showed his affection for me by giving me a ring. When Mom saw that piece of jewelry she asked me what it meant. I told her it was just a gift, no big deal. She said you don't accept a ring unless you want to marry the person who gave it to you. I thought about and agonized over that remark for a good many hours before I finally decided to return the ring to Pinkie. Although the ring was nice, and its giver was also quite a gem, I was not ready for a permanent commitment.

In helping me do research for this book, my son Marty was able to track down Pinkie who, like me, is an alive-and-kicking nonagenarian. He is still living in Milwaukee and we have started to correspond in Yiddish to each other. I have learned from his letters that his first wife, my girlfriend Gittel from the Yiddish folk shule, passed away a number of years ago and the woman he subsequently married is a practicing Catholic. His father would never have approved of such a union but Pinkie says wife number two is a *mensch* (a person of integrity and honor) and that's okay by me. Pinkie also writes that he works out three times a week at a gym. I'm not surprised. Pinkie always tried to keep himself in good physical shape.

Junior High and High School

I attended Steuben Junior High School, a former army barracks that when it became a school was named in honor of the Prussian-born American Revolutionary War hero Friedrich Wilhelm von Steuben. At Steuben, my civics teacher, Mr. Meyers, noticed my interest in wanting to help the downtrodden and suggested I consider a career in social service. In response, I wrote a poem in his class titled "Arise, Oh Social Worker," which foretold the vocation I would ultimately choose.

A central event in my junior high school years was coming across and reading *The Forsyte Saga,* a sequence of three novels linked by two interludes (intervening episodes) published between 1906 and 1921 by the British writer John Galsworthy. *The Forsyte Saga* chronicles the lives of three generations of a moneyed, middle-class English family at the turn of the twentieth century who have conflicts between the emotional impulse for love and happiness and the capitalist instinct for acquiring wealth. It is peopled by wonderfully interesting characters such as Jo, the philosophical outsider; Soames, the grasping man of property; Irene, who was "born to be loved and to love"; and Fleur, Soames' restless daughter. If one wants to read truly great literature of such merit that it earned its author a Nobel Prize for Literature (1932), one need look no further than *The Forsyte Saga*.

I received excellent grades in junior high and was the salutatorian at my ninth grade graduation, which Mom attended, as she was somehow able to get a ride to the ceremony. I eagerly looked forward to going on to Washington High School, an educational institution founded in 1901 that boasts notable alums such as US Senator Herb Kohl, the actor Gene Wilder, and baseball commissioner Bud Selig.

Unlike Sarah, who adjusted quite quickly to high school, I found my first few months at Washington High rather overwhelming in large part because I was only thirteen when I made the transition from junior high to senior high school. Many of the high school kids were quite sophisticated, some of them drove cars, some drank liquor, and some were even pregnant. Sarah had also become quite worldly.

Sarah and I were best of friends growing up. Being only seventeen months apart we thought of ourselves as twins, a whimsy Mom supported by sewing us identical blouses and dresses (our teachers were forever giving us compliments on the smart and stylish clothes Mom stitched). But our interests diverged when Sarah entered Washington High School one year ahead of me.

Sarah's elegance and good looks attracted the attention of lots of young men and she was invited to many mixed-sex parties. Sadly, I was not often summoned to such celebrations, as my acne and fallen arches impeded my confidence and capacity to socialize with members of the opposite sex. Sarah began dating and looking to a college career away from home, while I gravitated to my folk-shule friends and helped Mom with baking and cooking duties around the house.

Though we were engaged in separate activities in high school, the sisterly love that Sarah and I had for each other never faltered. We exchanged notes of affection when we were both learning to type and devised a private language to communicate that only we could understand. In the cookies of life, Sarah and I were each other's chocolate chips.

Speaking of foodstuffs, Mom was an outstanding baker and cook. Her delicious meat dishes, made from the choice cuts that Dad was able to bring home from his various butcher businesses, were nothing short of terrific and her apple pie, prepared with scrumptious-tasting Wisconsin apples, was second to none. But her pièce de résistance was Friday-night Shabbat dinner, which featured chicken soup, gefilte fish, fresh-baked *challah* (a traditional braided egg bread), and meat braised with potatoes and onions accompanied by carrot-and-prune *tzimmes* (a traditional

Ashkenazi Jewish sweet stew typically made from carrots and dried fruits). I looked forward to that flavorsome banquet all week.

I was a good student in high school and made the honor roll in most of my marking periods. I did very well in social studies, not so well in math. I took a botany course that I loved so much it made me think of pursuing a career in plant biology. But my biggest involvement in high school was working with the Labor Zionist *Habonim* youth group, where I was preparing to become a *halutza* (a female pioneer) and live with the *Yishuv* (the Jewish community in British controlled Palestine) on a kibbutz.

When I was fifteen, I went with Sarah to Camp Tel Chai ("Hill of Life"), a Habonim retreat in New Buffalo, Michigan, that aimed to prepare youth for a life in *Eretz Yisrael*. The camp was located in a rural, woodland setting, where we campers were required to clean our bunks and take turns at kitchen duties. But we also sang and danced, lit bonfires, had Shabbat celebrations, and learned and lived the principles of Labor Zionism.

Our Habonim counselors were idealistic and inspiring, as well as intelligent and broadminded, and I gained much knowledge from them about Jewish culture and what it would be like to live in the Holy Land. My parents were also smart but not as liberal as my Habonim counselors, so when Sarah and I came home from Camp Tel Chai we dropped the swear words we had freely used there. Mom and Dad would have been horrified to hear such language from their two "sweet and innocent young children."

(NB: Habonim was founded in 1928, in an impoverished area in the East End of London, as a Jewish youth cultural movement. Its groups were initially single-sex but were soon changed to boys and girls together. In 1982, Habonim merged with the Dror youth movement to form an organization known as *Habonim Dror*, a Hebrew expression for "builders of freedom." One of the main concepts of the movement's ideology is that of *tikkun olam* ["repairing the world"].)

Chapter 3

College and Graduate School

Wisconsin State Teachers College

I was barely sixteen when I entered Wisconsin State Teachers College (WSTC), now known as the University of Wisconsin—Milwaukee. Known for its innovative and experimental programs in teacher education, WSTC was nationally prominent when I went there and was considered one of the top teacher training colleges in the country. Golda Meir was a graduate of Wisconsin State (it was then called Milwaukee State Normal School) and afterwards taught in Milwaukee public schools.

I have a powerful recollection of an English professor whose poetry course I took at WSTC. She was a former nun who cried while reciting Christian-inspired verse, an annoying behavior that my fellow students and I were forced to endure on a weekly basis. I found her weeping out of place, as I couldn't relate to the subject matter in the poems she read to us and I had always thought poetry was about the words in a poem not about the person who utters them. But more than seventy years later she's the only teacher I remember from college so maybe there's something to be said for an instructor being overly emotive.

In my first year of college, the Yiddish folk shule hired a new principal by the name of Chaver Shapiro (*chaver* is a Hebrew word meaning "friend," sometimes used as a title for a learned man), a Hebrew teacher from New York who introduced me to the complexities of the Hebrew Bible and provided me with Hebrew language instruction.

Chaver Shapiro was a cultured gentleman and a learned and intellectual Jew. His appreciation of the classics was profound. He had season tickets to the opera and went to music and theater performances. He was also a member of the local sport and exercise club, which amazed me, as I had never met a Jewish scholar who cared about physical activities or working out.

Chaver Shapiro understood my intense desire to qualify as a Yiddish teacher but he made it clear to me that I also needed to acquire a much larger background in Hebrew, particularly in the area of Biblical literature. So during my four years at WSTC I diligently studied Hebrew, the Bible, and Jewish history with Chaver Shapiro.

Every Saturday morning I took a trolley to Chaver Shapiro's apartment and spent two to three hours receiving instruction, for which Chaver agreed to a payment of ten dollars for each lesson. He would often invite me to join him after our study session for lunch, a meal that might consist of exotic delicacies such as frogs' legs or Chinese vegetables. I was quite impressed that a middle-aged Jewish teacher had such sophisticated tastes, but not so awed as to respond to his long embraces before and after our lessons. Chaver Shapiro was seeking a mature love to which I could not respond.

When I finished my college classes in the afternoon I worked as a part-time primary-grade teacher at a Hebrew school. I met with my young charges for two-hour classes on Monday, Tuesday, Wednesday, and Thursday at four p.m. and on Sunday at nine in the morning. For their instruction I was paid the "princely sum" of ten dollars per week. I was immensely grateful for the job and the money.

When I was eighteen, filled with a strong desire to carry out the Zionist ideal of tilling the soil in the land of Israel, I attended Lost Lake Biology Camp, which was located in a rural area of Wisconsin now referred to as *Apple Country*. (When I revisited the area around the camp in the 1980s, free apples were available at all the hotels in the region.) Awakening time at Lost Lake was 5:30 a.m. and at 6:15 a hearty breakfast was served. Thirty minutes after that, we intrepid campers set off from our rustic cabins, which had been built under the auspices of a public work relief program known as the Civilian Conservation Corps (CCC), and trekked into the woods—with packed lunches and field glasses securely stowed in our knapsacks—to try to identify the vegetation and animal life of the region.

Mr. Throne, a high school science teacher and the camp's resident expert in biology, was tasked with answering flora-and-fauna-identification questions in his laboratory. What he was not tasked with was feeling up the girls in his lab, a job he seemed to relish a lot more than responding to inquiries about the native foliage and wildlife. Mr. Throne apparently thought the female students in his lab class wanted to learn about the idiomatic notion of "the birds and the bees" rather than the genus of such creatures. When he tried to get fresh with me, however, I quickly disabused him of such spurious reasoning.

The majority of the campers at Lost Lake were schoolteachers who went to the camp to satisfy in-service credit requirements. Many of them spent their free time, especially on the weekends, drinking and socializing at the local taverns. That's not what I did. I devoted my spare moments to soliciting donations from my fellow campmates to plant trees in Palestine, asking people to contribute to the Jewish National Fund, reading magazines and novels in my bunk bed, studying *Tanakh* (the canon of the Hebrew Bible), and dreaming of becoming a horticulturist in the Holy Land.

I double majored in education and sociology at WSTC and was preparing to become a public school teacher, a profession that had great appeal during the Great Depression, as there were job openings in the field of education. In my junior year, I did practice teaching with second- and third-graders and found I was reasonably proficient at the work. The following year my father encouraged me to accept a teaching position in Appleton, Wisconsin. But my mother and sister supported my desire to advance my education in the field of social work, which led me to apply and gain admittance to the University of Chicago's School of Social Service Administration in the fall of 1941.

University of Chicago School of Social Service Administration

The School of Social Service Administration (SSA) at the University of Chicago (U of C), the first university-based school of social work, was and still is one of the world's leading schools for the training of social workers and researchers in social welfare scholarship. It is one of a handful of institutions that helped create and define the social work profession and the social welfare field. And it is an institution I was privileged to attend.

Taking a train from Milwaukee and a taxi from Chicago's downtown railroad station, I arrived at the SSA with some of my belongings on a windy, star-strewn Saturday night in the month of September. My brother Joe and his friend Aaron brought the remainder of my wardrobe, books, and a radio the following day (I hadn't asked for a radio and thought listening to it would distract me from my studies so I told Joe to take the radio back home). On Monday I received my class schedule, visited the campus's Hillel Society, and strolled around the university grounds. I was tremendously impressed with the majestic setting of the University of Chicago, which stood in great contrast to the seedy South Side neighborhood surrounding the school.

Edith Abbott, the first US woman to become the dean of an American graduate school and one of the "founding mothers" of the SSA, was the dean of the School of Social Service Administration when I went there. She served as dean until 1942, emphasizing the importance of formal education in social work and the need to include field experience as part of that training. During her tenure at the SSA, Abbott also helped establish the Cook County Bureau of Public Welfare and in 1935 she helped draft the Social Security Act.

Dean Abbott occasionally delivered guest lectures to SSA students, some of which I had the good fortune to be present for. I also went to guest lectures given by Dr. Franz Alexander, a Hungarian-American psychoanalyst and physician who is considered one of the founders of psychosomatic medicine and psychoanalytic criminology. And I took classes with Charlotte Towle, a social work pioneer whose conviction and leadership in integrating the application of psychology throughout the casework curriculum and attempts to link psychological insights to the administration of public assistance transformed the discipline.

My first year's placement with the Chicago Department of Social Services involved me visiting clients at home and seeing the squalid slums of the Windy City. In the summer I took a job with Jewish Family Services in the Department of the Jewish Elderly, where I had the benefit of being conversant in Yiddish. In my second year at the SSA I saw clients at the Illinois Psychiatric Institute, taught Sunday school at the local synagogue, and worked as a telephone switchboard operator for the university.

While working as a switchboard operator I developed a romantic obsession with Mr. Harwood, a gentleman with a refined British accent whom I never met. Mr. Harwood said nothing about himself on the phone except that he enjoyed talking to me. But that, and his sophisticated British inflections, was enough to rouse romantic reveries in yours truly. To this day I entertain speculations that the mysterious Mr. Harwood was a suave and handsome nuclear scientist at the University of Chicago who was working with Enrico Fermi and other physicists at the college on the construction of the atomic bomb.

(NB: Much of the theoretical research for the Manhattan Project, a code name for the US-led program that developed the atomic bomb, was conducted at the Metallurgical Laboratory [Met Lab] at the University of Chicago. Under the leadership of Arthur H. Compton and Enrico Fermi, the Met Lab team built, and on December 2, 1942, successfully operated, the first atomic reactor in an abandoned squash court under the grandstands of Stagg Field at the University of Chicago. Enrico Fermi, along with J. Robert Oppenheimer, is frequently referred to as "the father of the atomic bomb.")

I dated a couple of medical doctors during my tenure at the SSA. One was a big fat fellow from Germany who didn't appeal much to me. The other was Dr. Boris, a brilliant piano player with a nervous twitch who took me out to dinner and then to his apartment. That date went nowhere and I was very glad to return to my room, which was the least expensive one in the dorm, as it contained the fire escape door for my floor and was farthest from the lavatory. But neither of those things bothered me and I was more than happy to save the money that more expensive accommodations would have cost.

My visits home tended to be sad ones, as Mom was battling intestinal cancer, Joe was working in Dad's slaughterhouse at a job he hated, and Sarah was unhappily pregnant in Madison, Wisconsin.

Sarah had met her husband-to-be Sam at a party she went to at the University of Wisconsin—Madison Hillel House. Sam was a nice-looking, bright, cultivated, chemistry student with a keen appreciation for classical music and a passion for opera. Their engagement was on, then off, and finally back on. It culminated in an exquisite wedding with the bride wearing a trousseau sewn by Mom.

After her nuptials, Sarah wanted to enjoy just being a couple for a while. But this did not happen, as she soon became heavy with child. That was a bad way to start what would prove to be a very troubled relationship.

Sam had depressive episodes that caused him to lose jobs and be hospitalized; eventually Sarah and Sam divorced. She then moved to California, married a tire salesman, broke up with him, and after that had great *mazel* (luck) with her third husband, Morris Goldsmith, a talented architect and the father of Jerry Goldsmith—one of the most prolific and successful composers in the field of TV and movie scoring.

Joe had *tsuris* (serious troubles) of his own. In his senior year at the University of Wisconsin—Madison (UWM) he was arrested for scalping tickets at a college football game. In those days scalping tickets was a much greater offense than it is today and the university summarily dismissed him from their rolls. Mom was devastated over Joe's big *shanda* (shame or scandal) and felt her son's life was over. That was far from the case.

Nobody thought Joe was a terrible criminal for what he had done and he spent the following year completing college elsewhere. He then went back to UWM and earned an MBA. When Dad asked him to do manual work at the slaughterhouse Joe agreed to the request despite the fact that with his advanced education, he was far more qualified to help run the business than push meat around.

The toughest part of going home was seeing Mom. Dad did everything to help save her, including sending his wife to the Mayo Clinic in Rochester, Minnesota, where the finding was inoperable cancer. I left school for a couple of months to try to assist Mom and be of comfort to Dad. I felt he could use a bit of cheering up, as Sarah was deeply dejected following her marriage and Joe had gone into the service, where he had a bizarre job for a Jew, that of checking to make sure Nazi POWs were receiving adequate and fair treatment. Dad insisted, however, that I go back to school and finish my education.

Joe met his wife-to-be Bette when he was in the military. Six weeks after their first encounter they were engaged. The two lovebirds courted through the mail. Sadly, Bette turned out to be a woman with problems. She loathed cold weather, so Bette and Joe spent their married life living apart—Bette resided in Miami and Joe in Milwaukee, where he worked in the real estate business. It was a tricky arrangement but they were both able to pull it off.

I wasn't sure what I was going to do after graduating from the SSA. Friends of mine like my dear comrade Avivah Zuckerman, a scientist pursuing a doctoral degree at the University of Chicago who later became a Haganah activist and a Hebrew University professor of parasitology, encouraged me to prepare to aliyah and be a social worker in the land of Israel. That was something I gave serious consideration to, but I didn't want to leave Mom. I also met a soldier whom I became very involved with, which ultimately made going to *Eretz Yisrael* an unworkable proposition.

How I Met Jerry

On a Saturday night in January 1943, I climbed the stairs to my second-story dorm apartment, pondering why my date, a medical intern who had just completed thirty-six hours of rounds at the local hospital, had asked me to go with him to see Chekhov's *The Three Sisters.* All the fellow had really wanted to do was sleep and that is what he had done during the entire play. After the show we quickly parted company, which was fine with me, as Doctor Drowsy wasn't particularly handsome or much of a talker. I looked forward to having a nice cup of tea alone in my kitchen.

As I approached my apartment I noticed the door was halfway open, which led me to think that the cleaning lady had stopped by and forgot to shut it when she left. I thought to myself, "I'd better talk to her about that in the morning. It's not safe to leave doors open in a dormitory. Someone could come in and rob the place." In fact, someone had come in—a soldier who was sitting with his legs outstretched on my living room sofa.

"Who the heck are you?" I screamed at this military intruder, "and how did you get into my apartment?"

He put aside some letters he had been reading, reached for his cane, slowly stood up on a bandaged foot, and answered coolly, "I'm Private Gerald Levinson and when it's possible I like to look over the girls I'm set up with before I go out with them. Since our mutual friend Rosalyn Shapiro, who arranged for us to go out next Saturday night, told me where you lived, I thought I'd call on you."

His New York accent grated on my Midwestern ears and his cocky attitude was the pits. It also didn't help matters that my underwear was hanging from a clothesline that ran from one end of the living room to the other.

"Look, buster," I told him, "I don't like men barging into my place without an invitation. Maybe they do that kind of stuff in New York City but in Milwaukee, where I come from, guys knock on the door before stepping into a lady's apartment. What kind of upbringing did you have? Don't you know you're supposed to ask a woman's permission before you enter her residence?"

He responded, "I do know that, and I apologize for the intrusion. But I rang your bell before entering and waited for somebody to open the door. When no one did, I tried the handle and, well, the rest is history. By the way, my mother would bash me with a rolling pin if she found out the way I came in here and my father would be mortified. And my sisters and aunts, whose letters I was just reading, would not be the least bit amused at my showing up here uninvited. I actually come from a very respectable family. Take a look at some of the letters they've sent me. You'll see, I'm not such a bad guy."

If my mother hadn't been so ill, which made me really appreciate the importance of a loving family, who knows how things would have turned out? But Jerry's reference to family gave me pause and I asked him how he injured his foot.

He replied, "Maneuvers. Tripped over some barbed wire. It hurts like hell, but the doctor says the prognosis is good. I should be pretty much healed in a couple of months." I said I hoped he'd feel better soon and asked to see the letters he had been reading.

The correspondence showed that his family clearly loved him: "I pray for you every night, Jerry." "Please take care of yourself." "We miss you terribly." "Mealtimes are so sad with you not around." "The Bronx is not the same without you." I decided to keep my Saturday night date with Private Levinson.

He took me to a chicken restaurant and seemed very impressed with my hearty appetite and love of desserts. I got a kick out of his New York wisecracks and found him a sweet guy with *sechel* (good sense) and a good head for numbers—Jerry had a BA in accounting from the Bernard Baruch School of Business of the City College of New York. We got married a year later at my parents' home in Milwaukee.

The Levinson Family

During the time we dated I took a train to New York City, a place I had never been before, to meet Jerry's family. At the train station in New York I was greeted by his father Louis, his eighteen-year-old sister Anita, his thirty-year-old sister Sylvia, and Sylvia's wonderful husband Nick, who liked to say, "Cast your bread upon the waters and it will come back sponge cake." They were all truly sweet people. When I told Sylvia that Jerry had asked me to marry him and had said I was more precious to him than his stamp collection, she said that it must be true love because nothing was more precious to her brother than his stamps.

I learned that Louis worked with his two brothers, Sammy and Jack, at a furniture store they all owned in the Bronx, the northernmost borough of New York City. He had first tried to make a living as a tailor when he came to America, and when that didn't pan out he went into the retail trade. Louis and his wife Ida also lived in the Bronx.

Louis was the indoor salesman for the Levinson Brothers Furniture Store (his brothers sold linens and other wares door-to-door in neighborhoods all over town). He worked six days a week till ten at night, staying home Friday evenings for Shabbat and all day Sunday. For pleasure, Louis listened to opera on the radio on Saturday afternoons and read the daily newspapers, of which there were quite a few in New York City, as many more papers were published in NYC in the middle part of the twentieth century than is the case today.

Like both my parents, Louis had journeyed to America from the Pale of Settlement. To escape service in the Russian Army, where men were being conscripted to fight in the Russo-Japanese War (1904-1905), he had fled his little shtetl town of Kalvarija in southwestern Lithuania to go to England. From there he took a steamship to New York City, arriving in the Big Apple in the winter of 1906. His future wife Ida, whom he had known as a child in Lithuania, had come with her family to New York in 1904 and was working in a five-and-dime store there. They met up with each other in Brooklyn, where they got engaged on March 1, 1911. Three months later they tied the knot and it stayed bound until their demise more than sixty years later.

Louis was a mild-mannered fellow who hardly ever raised his voice. His spouse had opposite traits; she was extremely excitable and a bona fide screamer. A domineering and demonstrative lady, if Ida liked you she liked you in a big way and if she didn't like you she'd trash you till the cows came home. I felt very lucky that Ida liked me.

Ida's in-your-face here's-what-I-think-of-you directness was a bit off-putting to me when I first got to know her, as I was used to a more diplomatic approach in dealing with people. But I came to appreciate and love Ida's sincerity and candor, and she became like a second mother to me in all the good ways that the term "mother" denotes. I felt the same tremendous sense of loss when Ida died in the 1970s as I did when my own mother passed on.

Louis and Ida had three children. Sylvia, the eldest, was a whip-smart, good-looking woman who attended Hunter College until the Depression years pushed her into the workplace full time. From her humble beginnings as a typist at a resident buying firm, New York's McGreevy, Werring & Howell, she rose to the pinnacle of fashion director, forecasting fashion trends and colors for stores like Marshall Field's in Chicago and many other emporiums around the country that relied on Sylvia's acumen to order their clothing styles each season.

Sylvia married her "prince," Nick Sissman, in 1935 and gave up her career in 1949 to mother her adored son Michael. A few years after Nick's premature death in 1954, she and Mike moved to West Hartford, Connecticut where she worked as an office manager, and the rabbi's secretary, for Beth El Temple.

Sylvia had great passion for all the arts—music, theater, dance, museums, poetry, books, movies—and was intensely interested in and curious about all aspects of life. She could discuss philosophy, politics, and art with equal verve and knowledge. I considered Sylvia a second sister and was deeply saddened when she passed away in 2006 at the age of ninety-three.

Anita, Jerry's younger sister, attended Hunter College, where she distinguished herself as editor of the college newspaper. Following her graduation she continued to work in journalism and became quite active in Jewish humanitarian causes, becoming the president of Hadassah in Southbridge, Massachusetts, when she and her husband Bernie moved to that city. Anita's interest in and commitment to Jewish philanthropic work and Jewish benevolent organizations has remained a constant to this day.

Anita was very bright—she went to Hunter High School in Manhattan, which was one of the best secondary schools in New York City, and in adulthood attended Hunter College and even law school for a while. She was also quite attractive, which can be a blessing and a curse.

Anita told me that sometimes when she took the subway train to Hunter, men would make offensive comments to her and rub up against her body. When Anita informed Jerry about her being harassed that way he offered to ride the train with her to deter such bad behavior—and he did. Anita also told me that Jerry owned a set of seventy-eight-rpm classical records that he was very fond of and would not let anyone play unless he was around, as they were made of shellac and so could be easily broken. She said his love for those discs had more to do with their monetary value than the music inside them.

Jerry was the middle child in his family and a bit of a rebel. He told stories to me about cutting out of school and visiting stores that sold stamps (Jerry was a serious philatelist), hanging out in pool halls, working for bookies, and delivering hops and barley for Prohibition bootleggers. Once, when he was caught leaving school without permission he was called to the principal's office, where his father was waiting for him. Before the principal could get two words out to admonish Jerry, Louis had his belt off to punish his son for his transgression. The only reason Jerry didn't get a sound beating from his father was because the principal intervened and said the school would discipline him.

But Jerry was also a dutiful young man who worked while going to school to make money for his family. He went to college at night so he could deliver cakes, breads, and rolls during the day for Pechter's Bakery, a New York City bakehouse renowned for their authentic Jewish rye bread. He also labored at other jobs to help sustain his folks.

Jerry was a superb athlete as a kid. He played shortstop on the Monroe High School baseball team in the Bronx and in his spare time shagged fly balls in Crotona Park for the legendary Hank Greenberg, a Hall of Fame baseball player who also went to Monroe, where he was an All City selection in baseball, basketball, and soccer.

Hank Greenberg, *aka* "Hammerin' Hank" or "the Hebrew Hammer," was the first Jewish superstar in American professional sports. He attracted national attention in 1934 when he refused to play baseball on Yom Kippur, the Jewish Day of Atonement, even though his team, the Detroit Tigers, was in the thick of a pennant race and he was not in practice a religious Jew. Hank is widely considered one of the greatest sluggers in baseball history and I am glad Jerry was able to make his acquaintance, even if it was only on the Crotona Park recreation field when they were both youngsters.

Jerry's *zaidah* (grandfather) Moshe Chaim lived with Louis and Ida when Jerry was growing up. An orthodox Jew, Moshe Chaim had strict rules for his grandchildren, one of them being that they attend religious services. To make sure Jerry went to such observances, Moshe Chaim paid him for singing psalms at the local synagogue.

Moshe Chaim also supplied Jerry with cigarettes, but not because he wanted to; Jerry snatched smokes from the open cigarette packs Moshe Chaim left around the house. On the rare occasion when Moshe Chaim caught Jerry pinching his cigarettes, he would whack his grandson with a cane and stomp through the apartment wailing that Jerry was no good and would wind up in jail someday. But Jerry said it was worth getting hit and chastised every now and again for taking his zaidah's cigs because the exotic foreign cigarettes his grandfather smoked tasted a lot better than the domestic brands he was used to smoking. Unlike Jim Stark, the recalcitrant teen protagonist in the movie *Rebel Without a Cause*, in stealing cigarettes from Moshe Chaim, Jerry was a "rebel with a cause."

Chapter 4

Marriage and Life in Brooklyn

War Bride

Dad did not want me to marry Jerry, whom he stereotyped as being "one of those fast-talking New Yorkers," a group he was wary of. He also did not want me to wed a soldier because "what will you do if your warrior gets killed?" But I told Dad that Jerry was a good man and that I loved him. I said I would take my chances he would survive the war.

Dad accepted my sentiments on the matter and on January 1, 1944, Jerry and I had a simple and charming wedding at my parents' house and afterwards a delightful reception at the luxurious and historic Pfister Hotel in downtown Milwaukee. I was somewhat sad on my wedding day, as Mom had died a year before and therefore I couldn't share my *naches* (happiness and good fortune) with her. But Jerry was very understanding of my feelings and the long lingering kiss he gave me right after we exchanged our vows helped relieve my melancholy mood. So did the bounteous breakfast he served me in bed the next morning with a single red rose in a vase beside it.

After we got married, Jerry was transferred to Boynton Beach, Florida, where he served as a warrant officer in the army. I was also employed by America's armed forces, as a billing machine operator. Along with lots of other women who went into the workforce to free up soldiers to fight America's enemies during World War II, I did my best to win the war on the home front.

It was hot as blazes in Boynton Beach, weather I was by no means used to, as I was raised in the frosty Midwest. One could try to beat the high temperature by using fans (air-conditioning did not enter the home of the average American till after the war) but they did a dismal job in keeping one comfortable in the scorching, summer Florida heat. To make matters worse, there was no bug spray around, so the insects ate you alive. But I was with my sweetheart and that made the adverse environmental conditions fade into the background.

I was also helped in dealing with the sweltering weather and the pests that faced me in the Sunshine State by my glass-is-half-full attitude toward life, an outlook that has continually assisted me in overcoming problems of everyday existence. Jerry's mind-set in dealing with things tended to be more of the glass-is-half-empty variety. Fortunately, between the two of us, there was always enough water in the goblet that we never got extremely stressed out or depressed in confronting life's challenges.

Jerry was eventually reassigned to New York City, where he did work auditing the books of companies doing business with the army. In the course of that labor he would sometimes discover that a company was cheating the military, whereupon he would inform the officers of that enterprise of his findings. Some of those executives occasionally tried to bribe Jerry to keep the information about their firm's wrongdoing confidential. Whenever that occurred, Jerry immediately reported the bribery offer to his superiors and told those who presented him such an improper inducement that they should be ashamed of trying to take advantage of the government, particularly in a time of war.

Jerry had an interesting military career. He joined the army a year before Pearl Harbor and was made an infantryman in the Ninth Division. Injuries he sustained in stateside maneuvers kept him from going overseas with his unit, a circumstance that probably saved his life as many men in his outfit were massacred at the Battle of the Kasserine Pass, which occurred during the Tunisian Campaign in February 1943.

Before I met him, Jerry had been working at Camp Van Dorn in Centreville, Mississippi, as the person in charge of booking entertainment for the troops and keeping finances for the post. It was a cushy job for a GI Joe and GI Jerry was most appreciative of the position. What he did not care for were the anti-Semitic remarks that some of the rednecks in his company directed toward him. To nip that situation in the bud Jerry challenged the biggest loudmouth in that bunch to a fight. When they finished clobbering each other, Jerry and his opponent shook hands and his rival told the other bigots in the unit that Jerry was a standup guy and they should leave him alone.

Jerry related stories to me about dating Southern girls who had never met a Jew before and were surprised they had no horns. He said he informed those women that Jews also don't have tails and cloven feet, information he believed they should know in case they thought that but were too embarrassed to ask. Talk about being *fermisht* (mixed up in the head, confused, addled, etc.)!

Jerry enjoyed his assignment at Camp Van Dorn so much that he kept declining requests from his higher-ups that he put in for Officer Candidate School. His bosses made those appeals because Jerry had demonstrated natural leadership ability and he had the highest IQ score of all the men on the base. But his supervisors did not push their demands, as Jerry was a highly valued subordinate who made their lives easier. However, Jerry ultimately agreed to go to Warrant Officer Training School and was sent to the University of Chicago, the place where we met, for instruction.

While Jerry was doing audits in New York City for the army, I was doing crisis management and casework in The City That Never Sleeps for the American Red Cross and other social service agencies. But I stopped all my employment in early 1946 to give birth to my first child, Martin, who came into the world on the seventh of March at an army hospital in Fort Totten, Queens. Jerry left the army soon thereafter, at which point we moved into a small one-bedroom apartment two blocks from Ebbets Field, the home of the Brooklyn Dodgers baseball team. We paid no rent for the apartment because a magnanimous and kind-hearted uncle of Jerry's, a well-to-do gentleman by the name of Mack Akabas, owned the building and he was fond of his nephew.

The Brooklyn Years

Jerry's first job out of the service was that of certified public accountant for Charles Hecht and Company, an outfit that supplied uniforms to the US military. On the side he ran a mail-order business selling ballpoint pens. I helped him with the pen peddling while taking care of my newborn child and maintaining our home in good order, which was never in good order enough for my mother-in-law, whom I loved dearly but who drove me up the wall with her *mishegas* (craziness) over keeping things perfectly neat. It got so bad that I finally told Jerry, tears pouring down my face, to tell his dear mama to let me run my own house and to his credit he did. From that point on Ida backed off from giving me housekeeping advice and our relationship, which actually had been rather good despite her incessant household criticism, became even better.

Three years after Marty was born, I gave birth to my second child, Daniel, on March 24, 1949. Now there were four of us residing in a one-bedroom apartment, which made for pretty cramped living. Jerry and I slept on a rollaway cot in the living room, and the boys shared the bedroom. When my daughter Judy came along (December 22, 1953), it was definitely time to go somewhere else.

My father had already gone to another place. Shortly after the war Dad went on a Farband picnic where he met an attractive redhead named Tilly, a woman ten years his junior. It was love at first sight for both of them and before you could say, "Let's get out of the frigid winter weather in Milwaukee and into the balmy California sun" they had gotten married and moved to Los Angeles.

Dad went into the real estate business in LA and Tilly became his secretary, his English teacher, and a cherished partner who helped his children feel welcome in a house she lovingly arranged. Tilly and Dad stayed happily married until she passed away in 1973. Dad lived alone for eight years after that before he too departed this life.

In the mid-1950s, our family moved from a one-bedroom apartment to a two-bedroom apartment in the same building where we had been living. That extra space came in quite handy, as on March 13, 1956, I was blessed with another child, my daughter Nancy. The four kids shared one bedroom (each child slept in a bed, or in Nancy's case a crib, against a wall) until we relocated to a house in Jamaica, Queens, in 1962. In the Queens home the boys had a bedroom, the girls had a bedroom, and Jerry and I had a bedroom. This was a living large situation compared to how we had managed in our Brooklyn quarters.

The apartment building and neighborhood where we resided in Brooklyn, which is now a New York City landmark historic district labeled Prospect-Lefferts Gardens, had many pluses. As my son Marty notes in his memoir *Brooklyn Boomer: Growing Up in the Fifties* (2011):

Getting to the park was a walk in the park, as Brooklyn's celebrated Prospect Park, a magnificent urban recreational area created by Central Park designers Frederick Law Olmstead and Calvert Vaux comprising a band shell, boathouse (with row boats and peddle boats), bridle paths, a carousel, a playground, 13 baseball fields, tennis courts, picnic areas, hiking trails, a skating rink, and a 12-acre zoo with elephants, polar bears, monkeys, lions, tigers, and a pony track where kids could get rides in a pony wagon, was positioned a measly two and a half blocks from our Lefferts Avenue abode. The Brooklyn Botanic Gardens, a 52-acre garden containing over 10,000 plant varieties, more than 200 cherry trees, a Japanese hill-and-pond garden, and a rose garden where one could lose oneself in, was a rhododendron's throw from the park.

The Brooklyn Public Library, which was located at Grand Army Plaza, was a leisurely twenty-minute stroll from our apartment. The library building, an architectural masterpiece with a long staircase similar to the one in front of New York City's Metropolitan Museum of Art had a 50-foot-high entranceway flanked by two enormous gilded-relief pythons, held all the books one could want or imagine. The Brooklyn Museum, an institution that houses one of the finest collections of Egyptian art in the world was a mere mummy's throw from the library.

A couple blocks from the house was the Patio Movie Theater, an art deco masterpiece with a highly gilded and ornamented auditorium and a goldfish pond in the lobby that people threw pennies into, where they showed double features. One could also walk to the Kenmore, Astor, Rialto, and Albemarle movie theaters, air-conditioned all. (Movie theaters were the first places to be air-conditioned in New York. In the summer, people regularly stayed at the movies the whole afternoon.)

Around the corner from where we lived there was a kosher-style Jewish deli where one could nosh on Hebrew National Hot Dogs topped with hot yellow mustard and sauerkraut, mountain-high pastrami and corned beef sandwiches served on real Jewish rye, large-cut French-fried potatoes, homemade cole slaw, baked potato—and kasha knishes; matzo ball soup, borscht, brisket of beef, kishke (stuffed derma served with gravy), latkes (potato pancakes), and sour and half-sour pickles. The standard beverage supplement to a delicatessen meal was a Dr. Brown's Cream, Black Cherry, Root Beer, or Cel-Ray Soda. Desserts were listed on the menu but they were rarely ordered because at the end of a deli feast a person was usually stuffed to the gills.

Next door to the delicatessen was Mom and Pop's Candy Store, a place where egg creams, malted milk shakes, cherry lime rickeys, and full-flavored vanilla and cherry Cokes were available from a soda fountain. Mom and Pop's also carried Superman, Batman, Sgt. Rock, Dennis the Menace, and Archie comic books; Topps Baseball, Wings, and Davy Crockett trading cards; Italian ices, Dixie Cups, Popsicles, and Breyer's ice cream cones; and an assortment of New York City newspapers, among them The New York Times, The New York Post, The Journal American, The World Telegram and Sun, The Daily News, The Daily Mirror, and The Herald Tribune.

There was a myriad of candies to choose from at Mom and Pop's and, as they were all so good and reasonably priced, selecting a particular candy was never an easy task. Nevertheless, it was a job one looked forward to because the payoff was so rewarding . . . Within an egg roll's throw from the candy store was a Chinese eatery where you could get a dinner for four that featured four entrees, two from Group A and two from Group B, for $7.95. Steamed rice was the staple, fried rice you had to ask for, and all the meals came with dark, dense duck sauce and hot yellow *mustard that could clear out your sinuses if you ingested too much of it.*

Crosswise from the Chinese restaurant was an Ebinger's Bakery, where delicious breads and pastries were sold. Ebinger's was famous for their cakes and pies. Although their pineapple crunch and butter cream had their fans the holy of holies was the Blackout Cake, a chocolate layer cake that was named for the wartime blackouts and filled and frosted with dark fudge and dusted with chocolate cake crumbs. Ebinger's also made super yummy crumb buns.

Jahn's Ice Cream Parlor was an ice cream sundae's throw from Ebinger's and when people in our environs hankered for an ice cream sundae, to Jahn's they went. Their piece de resistance was "The Kitchen Sink," the mother of all ice cream sundaes that could serve up to six. You could make a meal out of that gooey jumble of ice cream, chocolate syrup, whipped cream, maraschino cherries, and a whole bunch of other things, and when the kids visited Jahn's they often did. If you went to Jahn's on your birthday they gave you a regular-sized ice cream sundae for free if you had your birth certificate with you.

The Prospect Park BMT subway station was situated two and a half blocks from where our family lived, and the train fare was all of fifteen cents. The subway ride to Coney Island was especially interesting because the train ran above ground so you could view the different neighborhoods you were passing through. While some of those neighborhoods contained better-looking houses than the ones in the locality where I resided with my family, none of those residences matched our apartment building for its excellent location and the numerous things to see and do that were nearby.

With regard to our apartment building's excellent location, there was a grocery store around the corner that provided bicycle deliveries of food to our place once a week. A milkman left bottles in front of our apartment door and after we drank the white stuff he picked the bottles up so they could be reused. If someone in our family was too sick to make it a few blocks to the doctor's office our family internist, Max Blonstein, would come to our apartment with his well-worn black-pebbled-leather medical bag to diagnose and treat that individual.

After completing his visit Doctor Blonstein would often join me in the kitchen, where we would *schmooze* (chat) over tea and cookies, or maybe over a piece of pie or cake I had just baked, on what was happening in our respective families. Doctor Blonstein always had a lot more *tummel* (commotion, disorder) going on in his family than I did with mine and I would typically offer him *rachmones* (sympathy) for his difficulties, as I believe compassion is the best medicine.

In the fifties, nearly every doctor made house calls, a practice that became unpopular in succeeding decades because doctors did not consider house calls cost-efficient. However, house calls are beneficial in ways that go beyond costs; during a house call a doctor is surrounded with reminders of what all patients want their physician to know—that they are individuals who were not always patients. House calls make doctors more sensitive to the people they are treating. If I were in charge of health care policy in America, the first thing I would do is to bring back affordable medical house calls. But I digress. Let me go me back to recounting my life in Brooklyn.

In 1956, at the age of seven, Dan began taking violin lessons. He practiced in our apartment, and hearing him play the fiddle made me also want to study a musical instrument. As Dan's violin instructor lived in our building and came to our home to conduct his teaching, I decided for convenience sake I would take violin lessons with him too. Judy and Nancy followed in their brother and mother's footsteps by likewise studying the violin. Not so, son Marty. He didn't want to play a musical instrument. But I thought music training was important for children so I threw in a sweetener to induce Marty to take music instruction—after his accordion lessons I let him buy Chinese takeout food for dinner. After a couple of years on the accordion Marty switched to the clarinet and then took up drums as a way to drown out the "violin screeching," which he claimed permeated the house. But practice makes perfect and Dan demonstrated that when he switched to the viola and got so good at it he was selected to play that instrument in the All (New York) City High School Orchestra. Jerry, as the family impresario, paid for everyone's music lessons.

Every day after school, as long as it wasn't pouring rain or snowing, Marty and his friends played stickball, a street game related to baseball that was very popular among kids living in big northeast American cities during the fifties. The kids' field of dreams was the street in front of our apartment building. On that black-tarred, traffic-laden ribbon of asphalt they engaged in a sport that required minimal equipment (a sawed-off broom handle and a red rubber ball) and produced maximal enjoyment for its players.

I was always a bit nervous when Marty was playing stickball, as he and his companions did not always pay attention to the cars that whizzed by. Whenever I heard car brakes squeal I ran to the window to see if everyone was all right. Fortunately, none of the players was ever struck by a passing vehicle.

I'd often signal Marty to come upstairs for dinner by hanging a white handkerchief attached to the end of a broken bow, which had once been part of a toy bow-and-arrow set, out our fifth-story kitchen window. However, he frequently ignored my symbolic entreaty, which would sometimes spur me to shout from the window, "Your father just got home and he expects you to join the family for dinner right away. You better come up now if you know what's good for you." Those words usually got him upstairs immediately, as Jerry did not suffer fools or children who showed up late for meals gladly.

When I wanted Marty to pick something up from the grocery store for me and he was playing ball with his friends I'd yell out the window for him to get on the sidewalk to receive money that I would drop five stories to the concrete below. I engineered my money drops by putting coins or bills, or sometimes coins and bills, into an envelope that I sealed with scotch tape. I'd then wrap the envelope in a handkerchief, tie the hankie up tightly, and sail the entire parcel down to the sidewalk. If only paper money was involved I would often add a roller skate key to the contents so the packet would not blow around on its downward journey. None of my money packs ever broke open on the pavement, even though many of them were heavily laden with change. Unlike a lot of people who work in the world of high finance, I knew how to safely transfer currency.

On Friday nights, Jerry and the kids would gather in the living room to watch *The Phil Silvers Show, The Adventures of Rin-Tin-Tin,* and other TV programs that were on. TV-watching was a big deal in the fifties, a decade some have described as "The Golden Age of Television" because there were so many ground-breaking shows and ideas that set the trend for what people watch on TV today. All those shows didn't matter to me because I never looked at television, and still don't. I'm a busy lady who has no time for the small screen. But TV did me a favor on Friday nights in the fifties. It kept Jerry and the children engaged enough that I had moments to myself to think, make plans, and prepare for the weekend and the following week. TV was a Shabbat delight for everyone in our family.

Another family pleasure was visiting Coney Island, Brooklyn's Riviera for fun in the sun. There were amusement rides everywhere and lots of roller coasters, such as the world-famous Cyclone that no one in our family ever rode. Marty and Dan liked going on the Steeplechase Park mechanical horse ride, a full-size simulated horse race that took place on eight suspended double-tiered tracks suspended about twenty to thirty feet above the air that wound their way through the park's grounds and into the white-painted, glass-enclosed "Pavilion of Fun" Building. They also liked riding The Whip, an amusement where you sat two in a car that went along smoothly until you turned the corner, when it would whirl you about. I liked watching all the people in Coney Island having fun.

Sheepshead Bay, the community next door to Coney Island featured the Lundy Brothers Restaurant, a gigantic two-story California-mission-style eatery seating about 2,500 people and containing a 1,200-gallon lobster tank. Lundy's was renowned for their Manhattan clam chowder, Southern-style biscuits, blueberry pie, and fish. Whenever our family felt the urge for seafood, and Jerry felt up for a drive in Gypsy Green (that's the nickname we gave to the green Dodge sedan we owned—and the one I learned to drive on), it's to Lundy's that we went.

We also occasionally motored to West Hartford, Connecticut to visit Jerry's parents, who had moved near Sylvia when Louis retired from his job at the Levinson Brothers Furniture Store. A highlight of those trips was stopping at the Yonah Schimmel Knish Bakery on the lower east side of Manhattan to buy and eat their cherry cheese *knishes* (baked or fried dumplings made of flaky dough with filling [Yiddish from Polish *knysz*]), which tasted more like strudel than knishes. The kids looked forward to noshing on that delectable Jewish snack food as much as or more than they looked forward to seeing their aunt and grandparents in the Nutmeg State. But we usually dined at home and I enjoyed making and preparing meals for our family and anyone else came by to visit.

One of my more regular guests was Alan Weberman, a friend of Marty's who lived in the apartment directly below us. I sometimes gave Alan ham to eat and I could never understand why he took so much pleasure consuming it. Fifty years later I discovered, via an Internet posting, that eating ham was a turn-on for Alan. On his website he describes it as his first turn-on; his father, an orthodox Jew, prohibited non-kosher food in the house. Alan later experienced other turn-ons and, in the guise of A.J. Weberman, some celebrity by sifting through the garbage of folksinger Bob Dylan and afterwards writing a book titled *My Life in Garbology.*

Alan also enjoyed munching on the sponge cakes, angel food cakes, and chocolate cakes that I made, but those sugary confections did not have the same mind-blowing impact on him as the ham he was served. Who would have thought that a cut of meat from the thigh of the hind leg of a pig could have such a powerful, mind-altering effect on a person eating it? Not me, that's for sure.

Jerry Goes to Law School

Jerry had always wanted to be a lawyer but having to support our family with his full-time day job and part-time accounting work kept him from pursuing that goal. However, in the late 1950s he decided that, in spite of the time going to law school would require and the money he would have to forgo from leaving his part-time employment, attending law school made sense, as it would enhance his career opportunities and earning potential. And so Jerry enrolled at New York Law School.

Jerry went to school at night and studied on the weekends. Because I had more free time than he did during the day, I helped do some of the research and writing for his courses. We were a potent team and a family on the rise. *The World Telegram and Sun* captured our family's desire to better itself by publishing a photograph in their newspaper that showed Jerry sitting in an armchair surrounded by Danny and me playing the violin, Marty playing the accordion, and Judy and Nancy posing in ballet positions. Such erudition and culture! I wish my mother could have seen that newspaper photo.

On December 22, 1961, at the age of forty-seven, Jerry was admitted to the New York State Bar, which allowed him to practice law in the State of New York. He never did much practicing though, as he spent most of his life doing financial and accounting work. But Jerry had always wanted to be a lawyer, and a lawyer he became.

Joe, Sarah, and me (standing)

My high school graduation picture

Yiddish folk shule group (Chaver Shapiro is seated third from left, I am next to him)

Mom (left) and Golda Meir in Israel

Jerry and me in Chicago

Wedding day in Milwaukee

Anita (left), Louis, Jerry, Ida, and Sylvia

Tilly and Dad

Louis and Ida

Jerry, me, and Marty

The kids and me in Prospect Park

Jerry on Lefferts Avenue

Celebrating a birthday party in Brooklyn

Our creative young family

Our more mature family

With love –
Your brother
Joseph
3-16-68

Joe

Sarah

Jerry

The Grandchildren

Claire

Tamara

Hannah

The Grandchildren

Elisabeth

Jackie

Miranda

Yours truly

Chapter 5

Queens and Garden City

Going Back to School

During the 1950s, I did some substitute teaching in New York City public schools. I also took an acting class at Brooklyn College, where I had fun playing the role of Marie, a college art student with a strong and lustful appetite, in *Come Back Little Sheba*, William Inge's play about alcoholism, failed marriage, and broken dreams. And I attended Rabbi Abraham Kelman's *drosche* (sermon) sessions at the Prospect Park Jewish Center; I was the only woman in attendance at these get-togethers and because it was an Orthodox congregation I had to sit away from the men.

But for the most part I was happily engaged raising my four children as a stay-at-home mom in the fifties—a decade when bringing up children and housekeeping, as in prior decades, were considered ideal feminine roles. When the kids got older, in the sixties—an era of bra burning and the beginning of the feminist movement—I ventured out into the "working world," a phrase I take issue with because I think it demeans women who stay at home to rear children, which, as anyone who has ever done that knows, is very hard work.

In 1961, I took a job as director of community services for the United Epilepsy Association. Two years later I became the research director for the Health and Welfare Council of Nassau County. In 1966, I moved on to the Nassau County Health Department, where I was a staff supervisor in charge of information and referral services. I also began adjunct instruction work at Nassau Community College.

During the sixties, an opportunity arose for me to obtain a doctoral degree in social work at Columbia University on a National Institute of Mental Health (NIMH) scholarship. Jerry enthusiastically supported the idea but the dean of the Columbia School of Social Work did not want to admit me. He said I had been out of the social work field for more than twenty years and he felt such a long absence would make it difficult for me to understand and keep up with the class work at Columbia. My arguments to the contrary did not sway him from his position but Jerry was able to turn the situation around.

Jerry asked the dean to permit me to take one course and guaranteed if he did that that I would do very well in it. Jerry said he would pay for the course even though its cost was covered by the federal government's scholarship program. The dean told Jerry that instead of shelling out money for a course he should use that cash to buy me a mink coat because I was not going to succeed at Columbia. Jerry said he would take that risk and the dean allowed me to audit a graduate-level social work course, at the end of which I received an A and the dean's consent to enter the doctoral program. Four years later, in 1971, by studying on buses and subways that took me from my home in Queens to social work classes in Manhattan and through hitting the books at night, after making dinner for the family, and in the wee hours of the morning, before preparing everyone's breakfast, I received a doctorate in social welfare from the Columbia University School of Social Work. I was fifty-one when I acquired that degree.

The Queens Years

In 1962, our family moved to a house in Jamaica Estates, Queens, because we needed larger living accommodations and our Brooklyn neighborhood had gone into decline. The Queens home had three separate levels, a garage, a small backyard, and a working fireplace that no one ever used. It was situated on a busy street with a bus stop directly in front of it; the buses that stopped there traveled to a subway located a mile away. A city park, kosher

Jewish deli, Conservative synagogue, public elementary school, and a public library were within easy walking distance of the place.

Jerry Springer, a TV presenter who is best known as the host of the tabloid talk program *The Jerry Springer Show*, played guitar and sang songs one night at a backyard celebration at our house—a mutual friend of Marty and Jerry had invited him to perform at the festivity. Springer was going to Tulane University at the time and was visiting his parents who lived in Kew Gardens, a Queens neighborhood close to ours. I was told he did a splendid job plucking his guitar strings and crooning at the party.

Jerry's parents were Jewish refugees who had the good fortune to escape from Nazi Germany. Kew Gardens, where they resided and where Jerry and his sister were brought up, housed lots of Jewish World-War-II exiles in the 1950s. Survivors of Central Europe—Austria, Germany, Poland, and Hungary—they had left behind their loved ones, who would be murdered. Because there were so many Jewish émigrés residing in Kew Gardens it was colloquially known as "Jew Gardens."

I liked living in Jamaica Estates. One reason for that was in contrast to much of Queens, most of the streets in Jamaica Estates do not conform to the rectangular street grid but follow topographic lines, which gives the area a sort of country village feeling. Also, many of the named streets have etymologies originating from languages of the United Kingdom. Nomenclature such as Aberdeen, Avon, Barrington, Chelsea, and Chevy Chase Street sounded quite majestic to me. And I thought the name Jamaica Estates had a nice, refined ring to it, conjuring up visions of landed property with an elaborate house containing butlers and maids on the grounds. I felt a bit like a queen in Queens for the six years I resided in Queens County. And I felt equally regal when our family subsequently moved further east to another august locale—Garden City, Long Island.

Garden City

In the mid-1960s, I started doing adjunct instruction work at Nassau Community College and Adelphi University. I also began searching for a place outside of New York City for our family to live, as public school education in NYC had deteriorated to a point that Jerry and I were sending Judy and Nancy to a *yeshiva* (a Jewish educational institution), which was quite costly. I especially looked for dwellings on Long Island, a region where the public school system was a lot better than the one in Queens.

During my housing hunt, a colleague of mine from the United Epilepsy Association who resided in Garden City (a village in western Nassau County), told me of a house in his community that was on the market and suggested I see it. He kindly offered to drive me to the location. I accepted his proposal.

It was a lovely home within walking distance to two Long Island Railroad train stations and less than a mile from Adelphi. And wonder of wonders, though the house was situated in a very upscale locale it was one of the more modest residences in Garden City and so we could afford it. More wondrous still, Jerry agreed to buy the house even though we had also looked at homes in Great Neck that would have been closer to where he worked in the Bronx. But bless his soul, as I was doing adjunct teaching at Adelphi, Jerry wanted me to have the easier commute, so we moved to Garden City.

There were very few Jews living in Garden City when we relocated there in 1968. But there was a Jewish Center (that had members from all over Nassau County and even some from Queens) and I became quite active in it; attending services, going to Sisterhood meetings, helping to arrange holiday programs, etc. I liked the people who belonged to the Garden City Jewish Center and the warm, *haimish* (friendly or homey) atmosphere of the place. I also liked the rabbi, Meyer Miller, who had just returned to the US with his wife Shulamith after serving in South Africa for twenty years.

In 1985, Rabbi Stephen Wise Goodman took over rabbinical duties at the Garden City Jewish Center and how fortunate the Center was, and is, to have such an innovative, inspiring, and wonderful leader to head its congregation. Rabbi Goodman is also a good man and a true scholar. I learned a lot listening to the sermons he gave on the High Holidays (strictly, the holidays of Rosh Hashonah ["Jewish New Year"] and Yom Kippur ["Day of Atonement"]) and attending the *Torah* (the Jewish name for the first five books of the Jewish Bible) study classes he sponsored on Shabbat mornings.

In Torah study classes I read the New Testament and Koran, books I was not familiar with but works I found deeply engaging. It was interesting to compare and contrast these two religious tomes with the Hebrew Bible. The experience gave me a new appreciation for how important that latter book is to the core beliefs and narrative histories of the Christian and Muslim religions. As a lagniappe, I was also able to broaden my knowledge about the Christian and Muslim faiths.

During the time I lived in Garden City, I read many short stories by the Yiddishist Isaac Bashevis Singer, a man whom many people consider the best short story writer of the twentieth century. You can definitely count me in with that group. Singer's stories are clear and profound and are best read in Yiddish, though they hold up quite nicely in English translation. The following are some of my favorite quotes from Singer's writings:

- Kindness, I've discovered, is everything in life.
- Life is God's novel. Let him write it.
- We have to believe in free will. We have no choice.
- If you keep on saying things are bad, you have a good chance of being a prophet.
- Shoulders are from God, and burdens too.

I did a *bissel* (a little) gardening in Garden City, a community where many grand and gracious gardens abound. I cultivated hydrangeas, impatiens, and roses in my backyard and the tomatoes I harvested grew so well they were the talk of my block. I found gardening most relaxing and rewarding and eagerly looked forward all winter for spring to arrive. Then I could observe the new sprouts from the bulbs I had planted the previous year start to show themselves as they slowly crept out of the earth.

Jerry and the kids appreciated my gardening for its aesthetic effects and the food they were able to eat from the yard, but they didn't share my interest in horticulture. That was okay with me. My cares melted away as soon as I knelt in my garden, and the exercise I received from lugging bags of fertilizer and soil was as good as lifting weights in a gym. Getting down and dirty in my backyard was beneficial to both my body and soul.

Getting *bat mitzvahed* (a Jewish coming-of-age ritual) was also good for my soul. I did not go through a bat mitzvah ceremony when I was a youngster, which was not unusual for Jewish girls growing up in the 1930s. To remedy that situation I decided in 2000, as I was nearing the age of eighty, to have a bat mitzvah and I chose to make it a very special and sharing one by doing a twofold ceremony with my granddaughter Tamara Feld.

Our "double *simcha*" (gladness or joy) bat mitzvah service took place on November 4, 2000, at the Garden City Jewish Center. I read to the congregation from *Parashah Noach* (Gen. 6:9-11:32), a section of the Torah I had studied for months before to make sure I would do a good reading. When I stepped back from the *bimah* (the raised platform in the synagogue from which the Torah is read) after my recitation, I felt aglow with happiness to have finally been bat mitvahed and have my family with me to share my joy. Afterwards, a *Kiddush* (sanctification) luncheon was served for everyone in attendance.

(NB: The first public celebration of a bat mitzvah in America occurred on March 18, 1922 at the Society for the Advancement for Judaism in New York City. There, Rabbi Mordecai Kaplan presided over the bat mitzvah of his daughter Judith, who recited the preliminary blessing, read a part of that week's Torah portion in Hebrew and English, and then intoned the closing blessing. Today most non-Orthodox Jews celebrate a girl's bat mitzvah in the same way as a boy's bar mitzvah. Orthodox Jews, for the most part, reject the idea that a woman can publicly read from the Torah or lead prayer services whenever there is a *minyan* [a quorum of ten males] available to do so.)

Chapter 6

Working and "Retirement"

When I graduated from Columbia I applied for and won a tenure-track teaching job in the School of Social Work at Adelphi University. I taught there for the next nineteen years.

During my tenure at Adelphi, I was especially involved in researching and working in the field of information and referral services. I had been engaged in the field of I&R (the art, science, and practice of bringing people and services together, which is an integral part of the overall health and human services sector) since the late 1960s. At that time I helped co-found the Alliance of Information and Referral Systems (AIRS), an organization that has since become the national and international voice of information and referral. When I left Adelphi in 1990, I continued doing I&R work through grant funding and as a volunteer.

In 1984, I co-authored a book with Karen S. Haynes titled *Accessing Human Services: International Perspectives*. The following year, in 1985, I received a federal grant from the Administration on Aging to work on a program known as Senior Connections. This grant required the provision of information and referral services to the public by training older volunteers to learn about available services and resources in local public libraries in response to public inquiries. Over the course of ten years, from 1985 to 1995, Senior Connections became operative in thirty-eight public libraries in Nassau and Suffolk counties on Long Island.

In 1988, I authored a textbook titled *Information and Referral Networks: Doorways to Human Services* (a revised edition was published in 2002). Two years later I was privileged to receive

69

the Distinguished Services Award from AIRS for my contribution to the field of information and referral services. A year after that I received a Margaret S. Mahler Institute grant that is given by the Gray Panthers for intergenerational research and social change. In 1992, the New York State chapter of the National Association of Social Workers elected me "Social Worker of the Year."

I enjoyed my sojourn at Adelphi. I would have continued teaching there as long as my health permitted. But when I reached the age of seventy I was let go from the university because of a new policy that required faculty over seventy be terminated. That policy had just been put in place by Peter Diamondopoulos, who was appointed president of Adelphi in 1985.

Diamondopoulos also raised tuition and cut staff, which resulted in a precipitous drop in enrollment and with it, a steep reduction in revenue that brought the university into a full-fledged fiscal crisis. This monetary crunch was compounded by the fact that Adelphi's trustees were paying Diamandolopolous an exorbitant salary. The *Chronicle of Higher Education* reported that Diamandopoulos was paid $523,000 in 1993-94, which ranked as the second highest compensation among the nation's college presidents that year. Presidents at Harvard, Yale, and Columbia made $250,000 to $350,000 less than the Adelphi president.

In 1997, the New York State Board of Regents stepped in and dismissed the entire board of trustees. They then appointed a new board that ousted Diamondopoulos and hired a new president. Without Diamondoplous, Adelphi would have remained in good financial shape and I would have been on faculty there for a much longer time. Such are the vicissitudes of life. (NB: I was allowed to keep my office at Adelphi for a number of years after my "retirement" because the social work department thought I merited this honor. I also continued the Senior Connections program at the Garden City Public Library as a voluntary commitment.)

In 2008, the Board of Trustees of the Garden City Public Library presented me with a Certificate of Recognition on behalf of the residents of the Garden City community to thank me for my years of work with Senior Connections. State Assemblyman Thomas McKevitt likewise recognized my contributions to Senior Connections by giving me a citation on behalf of the New York

State Assembly. I appreciated the accolades from both these groups and was happy I had been able to perpetuate the life of the Senior Connections program beyond my retirement.

I also felt pleased when the US Senate, in 2011, approved Senate Resolution 241 designating November 16, 2011 as *National Information and Referral Services Day.* The intent of *S.Res.241* is to raise public awareness and recognize the critical importance of the Information & Referral/Assistance field. Support of the decree was published in the Congressional Record.

In 2012, I was granted the first lifetime achievement award from the Alliance of Information and Referral Systems. The tribute was a capstone to my forty-year career and interest in promoting I&R.

I am very grateful to have received the AIRS lifetime achievement award, and was thankful that my granddaughter Hannah Levinson was able to fly to the AIRS conference in New Orleans to receive the honor and deliver my acceptance speech. I am also appreciative of the many opportunities I have had to be productive and creative in life.

I have heard it said that life begins at forty (in 1937 Sophie Tucker recorded a song with that title and the German philosopher Arthur Schopenhauer said, "The first forty years of life give us the text: the next thirty supply the commentary"). But I think saying that life begins at forty, or that life begins at any particular age, is silly. Given that life expectancy has continued to move on, forty, these days, actually seems like no age at all. In 1991, the *New York Times* printed this observation: "All our age benchmarks, which used to seem solid as rocks, have turned into shifting sands. 'Life begins at 40? More like 60.'" Sixty? One can just as easily argue that life begins at seventy, eighty, ninety, or even one hundred.

Every day brings new possibilities for a person to learn and grow. And that is why I subscribe to the notion that life begins when you wake up in the morning.

Jerry's Working Life and Retirement

In 1950, Jerry started working in the accounting department of the S.W. Farber Company, a family concern that had been around since the turn of the last century and made highly regarded cookware. Two Farber sons and a Farber son-in-law ran the operation, which Jerry tried to help improve by giving suggestions on ways to increase the firm's bottom line. His proposals typically fell on deaf ears but he did not let that discourage him from passing along ideas on how to make the business more profitable. Jerry was a loyal employee who did the best he could to further the aims of the Farber organization.

(NB: Farberware began as a brand in 1900 in the basement of tinsmith S.W. Farber on the Lower East Side of Manhattan. The company made vases, bowls, pots, and a host of kitchen accessories. Farberware stayed ahead of the curve when modern appliances were invented. It was the first company to introduce the coffee percolator and an electric fry pan that could be submersed in water to be cleaned. Farberware is still in business and making various lines of kitchen products.)

During the Korean War, the Farber Company produced bazooka rockets for the US Army, and Jerry occasionally drove down to the Aberdeen Proving Grounds in Maryland to observe how those missiles performed. When the war was over Farber went back to making high-quality cookware and lots of money, as they rode the post-World War II prosperity wave.

The Kidde Corporation took over the Farber Company in 1972 and a great miracle occurred on the last day of Chanukah that year—the Farber family was let go. Jerry, who by this time had risen up the ranks to become a vice president of the firm, was selected along with two other officers to run the business. What a marvelous triumph for Jerry to have served so many years at Farber and to have outlasted his bosses.

In 1975, Jerry was named the first non-family chairman of the Farberware Company. He served for a little over a year before the executives at Kidde, who wanted to put their own people into top-level management positions, forced Jerry to retire from Farber at the age of sixty-three. He went out on top, though, with a good monetary settlement from Kidde and a Lincoln Continental as part of his severance package. He also left with his health intact, which I was very happy about.

Jerry had always liked to travel and in his retirement we did more of it, taking driving trips to Florida in the winter to stay near his sister Anita, a snowbird who allowed us to stay in a spare condo she and her husband owned in Delray Beach. On our motoring excursions I often slept in the car, a behavior that annoyed Jerry, as he wanted me to enjoy the scenery whizzing by as much as he did. But I was never the tourist Jerry was. He loved to see places and strike up conversations with strangers just for the heck of it. I was more interested in getting things done when it came to taking trips, like presenting a paper at an academic conference or calling on a relative.

Jerry also spent time going to the racetrack, visiting casinos at Atlantic City, and betting at OTB. He gambled very small sums at these venues. His real pleasure was figuring out strategies to come out a winner. He additionally hung out at the Fidelity Investment office in Garden City, where he closely monitored how his stocks were doing and kibitzed with other investors who were there.

Jerry, whose involvement with stocks dated back to his boyhood growing up in the Bronx, loved playing the market and did very well at it. In the last few years of his life he spent most of his days glued to the television set in our den, watching the fluctuations of the stock market on various financial channels. When he wanted details on a stock he would read me its symbol and I'd look it up on the computer. Jerry never shared any information about the trades he was making or his investment strategies. That was fine with me because I was interested in other things. I also had the utmost confidence in his financial judgment, which was heavily influenced by the worldwide economic depression that took place in the decade preceding World War II.

Living through the Great Depression had a huge impact on Jerry with respect to saving and spending money. In a nutshell, he greatly preferred the former activity to the latter one. Jerry was a big believer in the philosophy that a penny saved is a penny earned.

Despite his frugal way with money, Jerry was not parsimonious in his love for his family. He was always there in a crisis; early on in our marriage he saved my life when he instructed doctors in a hospital who were treating me for a virulent form of peritonitis to administer experimental antibiotics to fight the condition. He also agreed to move from an apartment to a private house because he knew I really wanted to live in a house—Jerry, who was used to living in apartments, would have preferred apartment dwelling. And he regularly sent checks to his sister Sylvia, and to his parents when they relocated to Sylvia's apartment complex in Connecticut, to help her pay the rent and get by. Jerry was a good provider who stayed at a job he did not really care for to make sure our family would have the means to make it in the world. When he passed away in 2006, he left a sufficient inheritance that guaranteed I would not want for anything in old age.

Jerry was an enormously talented individual who, sadly, did very little to put his mammoth skills gainfully to use in retirement. Other than doing a little bit of travel, monitoring his investments, and going to the gym at Adelphi once a week when he was in his eighties, Jerry did not get involved in outside interests or activities in his post-work life (he dabbled in philately for a while, but when the market for stamps went south for a few years in a row he gave up that pastime). And that was a shame because I think Jerry would have had a much more contented time in retirement had he been constructively engaged in further pursuits.

Old Age Is Not for Sissies

During the 1990s, Jerry complained of "drawing-like" sensations in his jaw area that were quite painful. He went to different doctors to try to get a diagnosis of his condition, but the best they could come up with was some sort of "Parkinson-like" syndrome. He also consulted the *Johns Hopkins Book of Symptoms and Remedies*, which Judy had given him as a birthday present, to try to self-diagnosis his problem. That effort proved fruitless. In the meantime, he suffered from a number of other aches and pains.

In taking care of Jerry's requirements for food, drink, medicine, and reassurance I became exhausted, contracted pneumonia, and was sent to the hospital to recover. While I was in a sickbed, Marty worked out a plan with Jerry to hire a full-time health aide to minister to his needs.

Jerry was a difficult and demanding patient; for a while we went through health aides like tissue paper. However, we finally found a very nice gentleman by the name of Abraham whom Jerry liked and who agreed to stay with us on a full-time basis. I still did quite a bit for Jerry, but with Abraham in the house I was at least able to get some rest at night.

Over time, Jerry's physical condition worsened. It was sad for me to see such a strong and vital fellow become debilitated and have to endure lots of pain. He was hospitalized a number of times for assorted medical ailments and eventually, when it became clear he couldn't be taken care of in the house, I selected a nursing home for him. He lasted in that place less than a month before succumbing to complications of pneumonia at the age of ninety-one.

Because Jerry was a veteran, I was able to obtain a military color guard to be in attendance at his funeral, and I was presented with our nation's flag at the close of the impressive and meaningful ceremony. We had been married for sixty-two years at the time of his death. It had been a real good run for both of us.

I wanted to stay in our home in Garden City after Jerry died but because of vision problems that kept me from driving, I knew I would need outside assistance to remain in the house. That external support materialized in the form of Pat Smith, a veritable *malach* (angel) who answered a help-wanted ad I placed in the *Garden City News* for a part-time shopper/companion. With Pat taking care of domestic matters I was able to continue to work on a number of projects that interested me, like attending Senior Connections library functions and compiling family-history notes.

When I fell in the house and cracked a few ribs in 2008, my children convinced me to hire a full-time companion, which I did through an agency. My favorite helper from the different attendants that organization sent me was Norma Ricketts, a caring and compassionate woman with a lilting Jamaican accent. Norma kept telling me that it was her job to help me to relax and enjoy my golden years, which should be the best time of my life. As I have always actively worked, and have enjoyed whatever work I was doing, I found the notions of "golden years" and "the best time of one's life" interesting but not applicable to me. I view all my years, even the most difficult ones, as golden years, and the best time of my life has always been the time I am currently living in.

My Philosophy of Creativity in Retirement

I believe that retirees yearn for something more than the quantity of time; it is the desire for a "quality of life." Significantly, retirement presents an opportunity to gain such quality through being creative.

A number of older persons have been highly creative in their advanced years. For example, Michelangelo painted the frescoes in the Vatican chapel at the age of eighty-nine. Benjamin Franklin invented the bifocal lens when he was seventy-eight. At the age of 104, Sarah Delany, a retired teacher, collaborated with her 102-year-old sister, Dr. Bessie Delany, a retired dentist, to write a book titled *Having Our Say: The Delany Sisters' First 100 Years*. The book became a bestseller and subsequently a Broadway hit.

The traditional concept of retirement is outdated. A more flexible approach to options and alternatives in one's senior years can open up avenues for creativity and productivity. The idea of vital involvement can benefit retired individuals and operating organizations, as well as advance society. While we formerly regarded retirement as the "beginning of the end," today we can regard retirement as "a new beginning." And retirees should make the most of their new beginnings because, to quote a familiar saying, "Yesterday is history, tomorrow is a mystery, today is a gift, that's why it's called the present."

The Levinson Library

Jews have long been known as the "people of the book," but Jews are also people who love to read books. That certainly has been the case for my family and me and to keep the tradition going, in 2010 I established and become the principal donor to the Levinson Library at the Garden City Jewish Center. The library offers members of the GCJC, scholars, and the general public access to Jewish-related literature, movies, and music for education, learning, study, and enjoyment.

Two people were highly instrumental in making the Levinson Library a reality: Rabbi Stephen Wise Goodman and Professional Librarian Deborah Rood Goldman. They helped establish an online web presence for the library and a means to expand its collection through purchases and donations. A dedication ceremony for the Levinson Library was held at the Garden City Jewish Center on June 3, 2011, at which time it was proclaimed that future library events would include book discussions, film showings, and musical performances.

Libraries have always held a special place in my life and I'm very thankful I had the means and opportunity to be able to found one. Libraries are institutions that contain gifts (of information, knowledge, and wisdom) that keep on giving and they are critically important to the progress and welfare of a literate and educated society. Wherever you live, support your local library!

The Most Recent Chapter of My Life

In 2012, after fainting and falling a couple times in the house, I had a pacemaker installed to remedy a circulation problem that was causing my weakness. When I was in rehab, I decided it was time to begin a new chapter in my life—moving to an assisted living facility. Being in such a habitation would offer me greater opportunities for socialization than I would have at home, and if a medical emergency arose, I felt the staff there would be better able to assess the problem and take care of me more effectively than a home health care aide would.

The first assisted-living place I tried was not to my liking and it specifically lacked an essential element for me—there were very few Jewish residents to talk to and no Jewish-related pursuits. Seeing these problems, my children got together and found a more suitable assisted-living residence for me, one that offers Jewish religious services, Jewish-related activities, and is predominantly Jewish. And that is where I am today, at Atria Great Neck; exercising and going to physical therapy and "news and schmooze" in the mornings, attending lectures and other activities in the afternoon, and receiving weekly instruction in the evening on how to use my computer.

I have a TV in my room at Atria but I rarely watch it, as I've got too much to think about and do. When I am by myself in my room I speak to people on the phone, or read *The New York Times,* the *Yiddish Forward,* or books that interest me, like the *Collected Stories of Isaac Bashevis Singer,* which showcases Singer's genius for storytelling. Having time alone also gives me a chance to reflect on what's happening in the world and what's happening in my life, two things I enjoy and take great benefit in doing. Socrates was right when he said, "The unexamined life is not worth living."

My Wonderful Children, Their Spouses, and My Grandchildren

Jewish grandmothers stereotypically brag about their children and grandchildren to whoever will listen to them. I fit that stereotype to a T, so let the bragging, which I will do in chronological-age order, begin. I will also be *kvelling* (boasting) about my two fabulous daughters-in-law and two remarkable sons-in-law.

Marty, son #1, worked for thirty-five years as a teacher, counselor, and administrator with the New York City Department of Education before retiring in 2004. He has published seven books, earned a PhD from NYU, and is currently president of the Institute of General Semantics. His wife Kathy has had successful serial careers as a dancer, actress, college professor, writer, and photographer.

Dan, son #2, is an attorney who has held a number of high-level positions in the federal government. To wit, he was chairman of the Merit Systems Protection Board and chief of staff for Congressman Bob Barr (R-GA). Dan presently is the Inspector General for the Department of Health and Human Services. His wife Luna recently retired from a high-level post at the US Department of Education. They have two children, Claire and Hannah.

(Claire is a graduate of the University of Maryland. She is presently working on a nursing degree at Johns Hopkins University after having worked in Medical Device Sales for St. Jude Medical. Hannah is attending law school at the University of Maryland. She has expressed interest in doing health-related law work and has already interned in that field.)

Judy, daughter #1, is a psychiatrist and the Associate Medical Director in Behavioral Health for the Independent Health Insurance Company. She is also on faculty at the University of Buffalo School of Medicine and is completing a masters degree, her second one, in medical management at the University of Southern California. Her husband Gregg is a radiologist and an avid skier. They have two children, Tamara and Jackie.

(Tamara is a graduate of Syracuse University. She currently works for Bloomberg L.P. as a bond specialist in San Francisco after having worked for Bloomberg L.P. in New York. Jackie is enrolled in a five-year BA/MBA program at Indiana University's Kelley School of Business, where she is majoring in accounting and finance.)

Nancy, daughter #2, followed in my footsteps and became a social worker. She has worked as a substance abuse and intervention specialist with the New York City Department of Education and is currently doing clinical social work with learning-disabled students at Adelphi University. Her husband Frank works for the US Social Security Administration and plays a mean guitar. They have two children, Elisabeth and Miranda.

(Elisabeth has finished her first year of college at Fordham University and is looking forward to the academic challenges of her sophomore year. Miranda is a junior at Mepham High School in Bellmore, Long Island, and is very interested in pursing a career in the arts.)

Kudos to my children and grandchildren! May they live long and prosper!

Appendix I

Memories from My Children

Marty's Story

When I was ten I went into a batting slump. No matter how hard I tried I was not able to hit a Spalding pink rubber ball with a wooden broom handle stickball bat. I became an easy out; as a result I was the last person chosen to be on a team in the street pick-up games that my friends and I looked forward to after school each day.

Stickball was the most important part of my life at that time, and my poor performance made me miserable. I couldn't concentrate on my schoolwork. I couldn't enjoy TV. I thought myself totally worthless. I longed for the two-sewer blasts I had always been able to hit, the solid line drives that careened off parked cars, and the adulation of my stickball-playing buddies. But I just couldn't hit.

One day, as I lay sobbing on my bed thinking about my failed athletic prowess, my mother walked into my room and asked, "What's the matter?" I could hardly get the words out through my tears. "I'm in a batting slump. I can't hit. I'm washed up. No one wants me to be on their side. I hate my life."

My mother flashed me an "I'll make it all better" look and then she said, "Everyone has slumps. Your father has times when he's not that effective at the office. I have bad weeks when it's tough for me to accomplish what I want to do. And Grandma, who is the world's best knitter, has days when she complains to me that she can't seem to get the stitches right. The trick is to keep on going and not get down on yourself."

Her words boosted my sagging spirits but her offer to pitch rolled-up balls of socks across the living room floor saved my life. For one week, in the late afternoon before my father came home from work, my mother threw sock balls to me in the living room, which I tried to hit with my stickball bat. To my surprise, I was able to smash those sock balls with complete authority. Lamps fell, the aerial was knocked off the TV, and knickknacks went flying as my batted sock balls found their marks. My mother said nothing about the damage I was causing. Instead, after each successful hit, she shouted, "Way to go!" or "Excellent shot!" My self-confidence soared. By the end of the week I was once again hitting two-sewer shots and my stickball chums were picking me first in the choose-up games on the block.

Some adults have fond memories of the toys their parents gave them or the trips they took them on. I barely remember those things. My fondest childhood memory is my 5'2" mother, who knew next to nothing about sports, pitching easy-to-hit sock balls and encouraging words to a stressed-out kid in a small Brooklyn apartment.

Dan's Story

In the 1950s, our family took summer vacations at Lake George in upstate New York. During one of those trips, when I was eight or nine, I fell into several feet of water in the lake and, since I did not know how to swim, panicked, and was rescued by Dad, who also couldn't swim. That was the triggering event in having me learn how to swim.

Because I hadn't learned to swim in summer day camp and was already old enough to fear the water, having me get swimming training was not going to be an easy addition to the family schedule. Nonetheless, Mom enrolled me for personalized swimming instruction at a pool located in the neighborhood of Twenty-Third Street on the east side of New York.

I remember it all quite clearly. Mom would leave everyone at home in Brooklyn, accompany me by subway to the Fourteenth

Street station in Manhattan, buy me a hot dog and soda at the Nedick's refreshment stand in the station, have us change for a local train to go to Twenty-Third Street, wait for me to finish my instruction, and return to the family apartment. It had to be an enormous inconvenience for Mom, but I conquered my fear of the water, learned how to swim, and was so excited about it all that to this day my chief form of physical exercise and recreation is to swim laps in a pool. I owe my lifelong enjoyment of swimming to my mother.

Judy's Story

When I was a junior at Boston University I decided I wanted to be a medical doctor rather than to continue as an art major. My father was shocked when I told him of my plan. "Are you serious?" he said, further stating, "Well, a biology major is good because you can do other things with it."

Dad was never thrilled with my switch in majors. I am sure he was concerned that being a woman would make the goal of becoming a doctor even more daunting (unlike today, when half the students in medical school are women, in the 1970s only twenty-five percent of med school students were female). Dad said I should give serious thought to becoming a medical technician.

My mother had a different take on the matter. She said there was no reason I couldn't be a doctor if I put my mind to it, and if being a physician was what I wanted to do she would support me all the way. Mom was as good as her word.

I transferred to Adelphi University to finish my undergraduate training. Because my mother taught there, I was able to attend classes at no charge. This made my father quite happy, as it saved him two years of tuition payments to BU. He also saved money on dorm expenses, as I lived at home when I attended Adelphi.

I regularly worked into the wee hours of the morning on my science experiments and my mother would often drive to the lab, sometimes as late as two a.m., to pick me up. During the car ride back to the house she would frequently ask me how things were going and no matter what I told her she always had a supportive response. Sometimes, when my experiments weren't panning out or when I found organic chemistry or some of my other science subjects difficult to understand, I'd become blue and discouraged and think I would never be able to reach the challenging objective I had set for myself. But my mother continually bucked me up, telling me to keep on persevering and that she had the utmost confidence I would get into med school and do well there. I felt I couldn't let her down, and I didn't. I finished Adelphi with a 4.0 grade index and was accepted to the University of Pennsylvania Medical School, one of the highest rated med schools in the nation.

My mother's love for learning and schooling continues to inspire to me. After finishing medical school, I obtained a masters degree in public health from the University of Buffalo and am currently completing another masters degree in medical management from the University of Southern California. To have a happy and productive existence one must live, learn, and grow. I thank my mother for imparting that philosophy to her children. It has definitely helped to make my life a more joyful and fulfilling one.

Nancy's Story

Thanks to Mom, I was able to share my adolescence with a wire-haired terrier named Terry Donuts. This canine was fun, affectionate, and very temperamental. She became the family dog for five years before retiring to a farm in Virginia with a family friend.

Mom purchased Terry because I was feeling frustrated and demoralized about our family move to Garden City. She felt having a pet would cheer me up. So she undertook a dog crusade to win over Dad with some minimal planning and the element of surprise. Terry was selected and purchased at a Puppy Palace store in the Roosevelt Field Mall on Columbus Day in 1969. Mom and I both had the day off from work and school. It was love at first sight (and bite?). When Terry came home with us that evening, Dad exclaimed angrily to Mom, "What did you do? Are you crazy?!" (He eventually got to really love the dog.)

Terry was a spontaneous non-research project, generated by maternal intuition and a very busy life. She managed to charm everyone between periodic mood swings, and worked her dog magic at a critical time in my growing up. Terry became a particularly cherished companion to Mom, especially during those early morning hours when Mom was working academically in the basement before the day unfolded. Terry lay at her side with her paws at Mom's feet, providing warmth and inspiration, as animals do when the love and care is then returned.

Appendix II

Memories from My Grandchildren

Claire's Story

I have so many fond memories of Grandma. One of my favorites occurred during the summer after first grade when my parents allowed me to stay with her for three weeks. This was so exciting to me because Grandma was my favorite person to play with. My hobby back then was playing a game called pogs—a game that involves using discs called pogs and slammers.

Grandma searched all day until she located a store that sold collectible pogs. We went to the store and must have spent hours picking out one-of-a-kind slammers and pogs, which she purchased for me as gifts. We went home that afternoon and played pogs for the rest of the day.

When I was with Grandma it was always a party. Whether it was a pizza party, an ice cream party, or a French toast breakfast party—she truly always made it a party. Nothing was better than sitting at the kitchen table, eating our favorite treats, and talking and laughing.

In my senior year of college Grandma, at the age of eighty-eight and in a wheel chair due to an injury she suffered a few weeks earlier, impressively showed up at my graduation at the University of Maryland to see me walk across the stage to receive my diploma. It meant everything to me to have her there to celebrate such an important day in my life. She will always be one of my biggest champions.

Tamara's Story

I have two serious loves in this world, family and food. So, of course, my memoir will consist of both.

Some of the best mornings I remember are waking up at Grammy's house to the sound of the train in the distance and the birds chirping outside my window; there must have been a nest in the evergreen next to the kid's room. I would wake up in my Tweetie Bird T-shirt that I never left the house without and wait until my tired eyes came into focus. Finally, getting my lazy butt out of bed (around 11 a.m.) I would approach the bedroom door. This was no easy feat, as Grandma's grandparents (really, really old people) were staring with an eerie intensity into the room from a photograph on the bedroom wall. However, my fear would quickly be dissipated with the thought of what was to come once I opened the bedroom door.

As soon as the door opened, I would rush down the stairs, grab a plate as fast as possible, and run up to the stove, where Grams was flipping the challah bread in the pan. It was Grandma's French toast, a total extravagance I looked forward to and, other than her wonderful company, was the best part about visiting her. I would put in my request for three large pieces and try to not fidget while I waited for that delicious smell to appear as a physical and edible form on my plate. Once it finally did, I took the maple syrup and poured rivers of it onto my dish. I ate each piece individually to get the greatest syrup–to-challah ratio possible. I even ate the burnt part, which was a big faux pas when I did it at home.

When Grams had made enough to feed everyone in the family, she would sit down and eat a piece (usually with her hands) and we would sing "Toast, toast, toast, that's what I like the most. Toast, toast, toast, that's what I want the most." She would clap her hands as we sang and ate together as a family. Despite the sugar rush from the mounds of added maple syrup, food coma would eventually hit and we would all retire to the comfy couches in the living room. Grams would sit in the blue chair facing the horizontally laying family and we would talk about the day and the work she had to do on her book. Breakfasts followed by these morning relaxations are recollections I will cherish forever.

Grams, I love you so much. This is just one of the many memories I have of you. Our joint bat mitzvah, your birthdays, holidays, and just lounging around together have all been amazing and will remain with me eternally. I miss you and love you and cannot wait to see you soon!

Hannah's Story

It is difficult to reduce to a few sentences all the loving memories that I have of Grandma. I will focus on the recurring memory I have of her, one of my fondest times as a child, Grandma's invention of the "girl's party."

Girl's party was the Friday evening celebration in her kitchen where members of the male sex were not allowed. It was an occasion to create the most exotic desserts, including multiple flavors of ice cream with cookies on top, sprinkles, marshmallows, and more.

How cool it was to have my grandmother shooing my father out of the kitchen as she began to set up the mounds of sugar that we would soon ingest. Dad was inevitably hopeless in his protests about healthy eating. This was my sister Claire's and my reward for traveling five hours in the car from Washington, DC to spend the weekend in New York.

The time that Claire and I spent in Grandma's kitchen, eating until we almost passed out on the table, was unbelievably exciting. Aside from the endless games that Grandma always played with us, she never told us to "stop eating" or "balance the meal with something healthy." My very own Jewish Paula Dean! Grandma's warm, heartfelt (and delicious) greetings set the tone for the entire weekend and kept us begging dad to let us visit her more.

Jackie's Story

When I was about 11 years old, Grams gave all the girls in the family diamond horseshoe necklaces. I fell in love with my necklace and found it to be a very special connection to the Levinson side of the family. I have worn it practically every day since it was given to me and currently still wear it every day. I never take it off. I work out, shower, and sleep in it. If I do not have it on I feel like something is missing. I love when people ask me about it and I am able to tell them about how my grandma gave it to me for good luck (because of the horseshoe shape) when I was a lot younger and it has brought me good luck ever since.

When I got older Grams gave me the most stunning diamond ring I have ever seen. This was a very special moment for me because Grams did it in an extremely private and meaningful setting. She sat me down in her bedroom, pulled a box out of her bottom drawer, and from that box took out a sparkling diamond ring. She told me it was her stepmom Tilly's (my great grandmother's) and it was very special to her. She wanted me to have it because I love going to the theater and she believed I could wear it on more elegant theater outings when I dressed up. I keep this ring locked up, unlike the horseshoe necklace, and only wear it on very special occasions.

Both these pieces of jewelry have had a huge impact on my life. I enjoy them even more because I know I can have them forever, and thus a piece of Grams is always with me. I intend to continue wearing articles of jewelry until I am Gram's age. Then I too can pass them down to my children and grandchildren and hopefully give them the same connected and loved feelings that I felt when I received them.

Elisabeth's Story

When I was due to start my freshman year at Fordham University, I was beyond nervous. It was a new experience, a new adventure, but also foreign and unknown, and therefore scary. Living with Grandma completely saved me.

When I asked Grams if I could stay with her, she was so excited and welcoming. I came over and she had made up the bed for me. Knowing that she was home waiting for me every day was such a boost. No matter how crazy my studies became or how bad my day was, Grandma made everything better when she gleefully asked, "How was school?" She was interested in every assignment that I had, and I always printed out two copies of everything, one of which went into a special blue binder for her review.

I got to spend more time with Grandma than ever before. We spent hours talking about me, and about her. I helped her organize her papers and we looked at her treasures together. She read her mother's letters to me, and I finally gained an understanding of what "Information and Referral" actually meant.

When I was stressed out about an inconceivably difficult philosophy paper that I had only a few days to write, Grams gave me a soft pink robe of hers to wear. I didn't take it off until I had finished the last page.

We spent Chanukah together. I brought the menorah and the candles, and she sang "Chanukah Oy Chanukah" in Yiddish. For New Year's I convinced Grandma to watch *It's a Wonderful Life* with me on the computer, and she eventually concluded that it was indeed a very nice story.

I will always cherish the special time that we had when I was a resident at Lincoln Street, and I will always associate Grams with my freshman year.

Miranda's Story

On the eve of January 1st, 2009, my parents dropped me off at my first ever New Year's Eve bash. As I left the car, I noticed the snow had already accumulated up to my knees, this being the big blizzard of January 2009. I said my goodbyes and was greeted at the front door by an acquaintance of mine, a shallow girl whom I had made fast friends with upon arriving at a new school. Inviting me to her large family's New Year's Eve party had been her idea, a way to ward off boredom while all of the adults were drinking champagne and talking noisily. I felt like an outsider there, but was flattered by the invitation, having spent the past eleven New Year's Eves of my life watching the ball drop on television, with my parents.

"Want to sleep over?" she asked me. The minute I said "Yes" I knew it was the wrong answer. I missed my parents and felt isolated, being surrounded by strangers. We spent the evening counting down the hours till midnight with the neighborhood kids from down the block, while I nervously thought of ways to avoid sleeping over. By one o' clock in the morning, it was too late. My hostess was deep in sleep, and I was a mess, tossing and turning. I took out my phone and began dialing my parents; however, getting a call at three a.m. would infuriate my dad so I cancelled the call. I didn't want to be chastised for my bad decision-making, and I needed a comforting voice. I dialed my grandma.

"Hello?" she answered the phone before it had even rung twice.

"Grandma?" I whispered. "Happy New Year." We chatted quietly before I told her the real reason I had called at this hour. When I apologized for the inconsideration of calling her in the middle of the night she was quick to correct me.

"You can always call me. Morning, noon, or night." It was as simple as that. We hung up, and I fell asleep instantly.

Appendix III

Three Philosophical Inquiries

Can a Woman Have it All?

No one can have it all. But I have had a lot, to wit, a long-lasting marriage of sixty-two years, four children and six grandchildren, a highly satisfying family life, and an engaging and productive career. How did this all happen? Through focus, determination, personality, and luck.

I believe if one wants something in life one should be ready and willing to work for it. I wanted a happy married life and I achieved that through diligent effort and compromise with my husband. Part of the diligent effort involved taking care of all the household chores in our family—in all the years we were married Jerry never did the laundry, washed a dish, or mopped the floor. Did I resent having to do such mundane tasks without assistance from my partner? No, I did not. In my generation it was expected that women would take care of domestic responsibilities. As to compromise with my spouse, I have always tried to look at the bright side of things and find common ground on matters where principle is not involved. Those attitudes helped me in coming up with negotiated decisions that Jerry and I could both live with.

Child-raising was something I very much enjoyed and I was fortunate that when I brought up my children the role of stay-at-home mother was part of the zeitgeist, so there was no social pressure for me to do anything else. And when I wanted to do something else, specifically get a graduate degree and pursue a career, those aspirations were also part of the spirit of the times in the era when I made those choices.

With respect to vocational achievement, like Thomas Edison, who was able to function on three to four hours of sleep a night, I also don't need much sleep to get by on. Having additional hours of wakefulness gave me more time than most people to accomplish what I set out to do. I also do not watch TV, so I didn't lose time vegetating in front of the tube. (My outlook on TV is simple: if you want to be involved with television be *on* a program rather than passively view one as a spectator.) And, unlike people who complain that they do not have enough hours in the day to accomplish what they wish, I believe if you really desire to achieve something you can find a way to manage your time to do it. At the tender age of ninety-two I still subscribe to that philosophy.

Why Israel?

The story of the Jews in the days of the Pharaohs is a good model for most of the Jewish exiles that followed. The Jews are invited in as guests, make considerable contributions, and then are enslaved or killed. Moses, the Jewish Abraham Lincoln, ultimately liberated the slaves and led the Jews out of Egypt. From there they, but not Moses, made it to the land of milk and honey where Solomon built a temple that the Babylonians under King Nebuchadnezzar II destroyed in 586 BCE.

When the Persian Empire followed the Babylonians, the Jews were almost completely wiped out through the machinations of Haman, the advisor to King Ahasuerus. Luckily, Queen Esther, the Jewish wife of Ahasuerus, was able to save her people and, miracle of miracles, Haman was hung.

When Hellenism began to impose itself by force, the Jews responded with the rebellion of the Maccabees in 164 BCE and a rededication of the Temple, which produced the miracle of Chanukah with the oil to light the candles lasting longer than naturally possible.

The Romans were sadistic and persecuted the Jews. The most famous example of that maltreatment was the crucifixion of a Jew named Jesus. The Romans also torched Jerusalem and the

Second Temple, leaving only the Western Wall, in 70 CE. And they massacred the Zealots at Masada.

From the time Christianity was declared the state religion of the Byzantine Empire by Constantine the Great in the fourth century, hatred of the Jews became national policy in Christian lands and a hyper fixation. "Blood libels" (false accusations that Jews murder Gentile children to obtain ritual blood, especially for Passover matzos) and baseless charges of child killing led Jews to be sentenced to death by various authorities. Between 1290 and 1497 the Jews were expelled from Britain, France, Spain, Portugal, and other places.

The Black Plague, a devastating pandemic that killed off many of the inhabitants of Europe between 1348-1350 was blamed on the Jews, those "vile and despicable Christ-killers." Worse yet, in 1648 Cossack nationalists from the Ukraine butchered one half the total Jewish population of the Ukraine and Galicia; a carnage so ghastly that some historians view it as a preview of the Holocaust.

The French Revolution in the late eighteenth century ushered in a new age of freedom and equality for the Jews that paved the way for similar movements in the rest of Europe. But good feelings toward Jews were set aside with the trial of Alfred Dreyfus, a Jewish captain in the French army, who was wrongly accused of treason. Moved by the anti-Semitism that led to and was publicly proclaimed during the Dreyfus trial, Theodore Herzl, a Jewish Austro-Hungarian journalist and playwright, became obsessed with Zionism—an international political movement devoted to creating a Jewish state in Palestine. Herzl successfully convened the First Zionist Congress in 1897. Twenty years later, Zionism gained added impetus through a letter from the United Kingdom's Foreign Secretary, Arthur James Balfour, to Baron Rothschild, a leader of the British Jewish community.

The Balfour Declaration stated that the British government viewed positively the establishment in Palestine of a national home for the Jewish people. That avowal led to an increased emigration of Jews to Palestine and an increase in Arab atrocities against Jewish settlers, such as the Hebron Massacre in 1929 that killed sixty-seven Jews. Then came World War II, which brought with it the *Final Solution*.

The Final Solution was Nazi Germany's plan for and execution of the systematic genocide of European Jews during World War II, resulting in the most deadly phase of the Holocaust. This decision to systematically kill the Jews of Europe was made either by the time of or at the Wannsee Conference, which took place in Berlin on January 20, 1942. Almost six million European Jews were eradicated through state-sponsored Nazi murder during World War II.

The world shares a measure of guilt with Nazi Germany for its silence, its passivity, and sometimes—as when the S.S. St. Louis was not allowed to land Jewish refugees from Germany in the United States in 1939 (the refugees on board were sent back to Germany to be murdered)—its direct involvement in the Jewish genocide orchestrated by Adolph Hitler.

In the summer of 1947, the *Exodus,* a ship carrying thousands of Holocaust survivors, was not permitted to land in Palestine but was sent back by the British to Europe. That decision, to return people displaced by Nazi atrocities to the place where such atrocities occurred, roused the world's conscience and helped bring an end to British control over Palestine.

On November 29, 1947, Jews around the world celebrated when the United Nations voted Israel into existence. Against the "nays" of all the Arab states, the UN voted to partition Palestine into Jewish and Arab sections. Jews reveled over the right they were given to a small bit of land. The Arabs rejected the plan and seven Arab nations attacked Israel. That was the agony, but the ecstasy was in the offing. The Israelis were able to fend off their antagonists and maintain their state, both of which they have had to continue to do. And Israel will keep on defending itself from those who seek her demise, for history shows that the world has often been less than kind to the Jewish people, a group that clearly needs a safe haven to shield itself from murder and misfortune.

Are there Words of Wisdom that Can Help One to Achieve a Happy and Productive Life?

Yes there are, and I have listed some of them on the next page. If you want to live a happy and productive life I suggest putting these words into practice. Doing that has worked for me.

"Who refreshes others will be refreshed."
    Book of Proverbs

"If I am not for myself who will be for me? And if I am only for myself, what am I? And if not now, when?"
"That which is hateful to you do not do to your fellow. That is the whole Torah; the rest is commentary."
    Hillel

"Whosoever destroys a soul, it is considered as if he destroyed an entire world. And whosoever that saves a life, it is considered as if he saved an entire world."
    The Talmud

"In the Lord put your trust."
    Book of Psalms

"For wisdom is a defense, and money is a defense: but the excellency of knowledge is, that wisdom giveth life to them that have it."
    Ecclesiastes

Appendix IV

Aging and Time-Binding in the Twenty-First Century

The following is an article I published in *ETC: A Review of General Semantics* (Vol. 60, No. 1, 2003). The central point of the piece is that with increased longevity, and the chance to be creative in advanced age, older persons have an opportunity to become more valuable transmitters of knowledge to future generations, thus contributing to a richer and more advanced human culture. I believe society and individuals can help older persons realize that opportunity by encouraging them to engage in creative pursuits and to interact more with younger people. Such efforts would be beneficial to all parties involved and, barring catastrophic events, make the twenty-first century the most notable so far in the history of human *time-binding* (a general semantics notion involving the characteristic human ability, using language and other symbols, to transmit information across time).

AGING AND TIME-BINDING IN THE TWENTY-FIRST CENTURY

The concept of "time" has a wide range of meanings and is applied to highly diverse settings. For example, prisoners serve time, musicians mark time, idlers pass time, referees call time, historians record time, and scorekeepers keep time (Greenberg, 1990). The Scriptures maintain, "To everything there is a season—a time to be born, and a time to die, a time to kill and a time to heal, a time to love and a time to hate . . ." (Ecclesiastes, 3). Thus, time is assigned to a specific task or a predetermined event in accordance with a specific purpose. This article will explore different ideas related to how seniors can improve the way they spend time and maximize their positive impact on the next generation—in other words, how seniors can become better time-binders.

An Aging Society—Socio-Demographic Trends and Time-Binding Opportunities

The general semantics formulation, time-binding, concerns our human ability to use language and other symbols to store and pass on knowledge, so that each new generation can benefit from earlier discoveries and start from where the previous generation left off.

The concept of time-binding has assumed special significance in view of the unprecedented expansion of the aging population. Demographic forecasts predict that the aging population will continue to increase significantly in the twenty-first century. America is steadily growing older as more people are living longer and more are celebrating their centenarian birthdays. It is predicted that by 2030, one out of every five persons (20%) will be over 60 years old (Hooyman and Kiyak, 1996). Moreover, as the 75 million baby boomers that were born between 1946 and 1964 "come of age," the number of older persons will significantly increase into what has been described as an "age wave" and a "gerontocracy."

Another significant demographic trend is the increase of multigenerational families, which may include four- and five-generation families. This growing phenomenon is a consequence of extended longevity, in addition to higher divorce rates and remarriages, since the longer the members of a particular generation live on, the more likely it is that they will be living among subsequent generations. Consequently, opportunities for time-binding will multiply as younger and older generations engage in time-sharing.

In our post-industrial (or post-modern) society, research no longer focuses exclusively on the pathology associated with aging, nor exclusively on what is possible despite aging. It also investigates what is possible because of aging, given the potential and opportunity for creativity during the advanced years. There is no denial of the "problems" that occur in later life. However, research is focusing more on the possibilities, the strengths, and the opportunities of intergenerational sharing.

Longevity has heralded a new era of shared opportunities for intergenerational time-binding. Older volunteers are engaged as readers and storytellers in elementary schools, as career counselors and tutors in high schools, and as associates in colleges. Older and younger volunteers share hours of community service in local neighborhoods as well as in health facilities. Children are teaching English to their newly arrived ethnic grandparents, and they provide instruction in computer science to their parents. Grandparents are increasingly assuming responsibility for childcare in working families as well as in homes of divorced parents. The proverbial "empty nest" is intermittently filled with adult children returning to live with aging parents or grandparents. These time-sharing experiences provide transmission of intergenerational values and culture that extend beyond the lifetime of individual family members.

Cultural Attitudes Toward Aging

In various traditional societies such as Asian and Biblical cultures, older persons tend to be regarded with reverence, and are often respected as "visionaries" and "persons of wisdom" in the transmission of culture from generation to generation. In contrast to these positive and respected roles of older persons, a bias against aging persists in our modern society, which Robert Butler (1969), renowned geriatrician, identified as "ageism." This type of negativism and rejection of older persons is based on a form of social discrimination and prejudice against older adults. Ageism stems from a belief that aging causes people to become dysfunctional and incapable of productive work and retraining. While current legislation formally prohibits age discrimination, ageism tends to persist in subtle as well as in overt situations.

One society's response to ageism has been the development of a vast multimillion dollar industry that is aimed at helping people "look younger" and to "melt away the years" with the aid of face lifts, miracle diets, liposuction operations, hair restoration, extensive and expensive "anti-aging" cosmetics, and countless devices and remedies to "restore that youthful image" (Hooyman, 1996).

A Look at Labeling

Benjamin Franklin wisely observed, "What signifies knowing the names if you know not the 'nature of things?'" How we determine and label who is "old" seems problematic and contradictory. In observing nature, one does not necessarily refer to natural processes as "aging." We do not say a sunflower grows older. We can say that it "ripens," it drops its seeds, and the cycle goes on within the "ripening process." Therefore, might we call the process of humans moving through time a process of "ripening"?

There is no shortage of terms used to describe older persons. Some generally acceptable terms refer to older adults as "retirees," "senior citizens," "golden agers," and "pensioners." However, other labels can carry a sharp sting, for example, "geezer," "old hen," "fossil," or "old fogey." A new set of descriptions has evolved that tends to view older persons as "cool," and "really with it." We also see more commercial images of well-tanned older people who play tennis, dance, jog, work out or lift weights, and are "sexually active."

The degree of aging of older persons may also be assessed by one's capacity to operate with various degrees of bodily movement, which can be postulated as a "go-go theory of aging." The initial "go-go" condition may over time become "go slow," followed by "slow go," "cannot go," and eventually "no." And how about the value-laden, controversial term that labels older adults as "chronologically gifted"?

Beyond Categorizing the Human Life Span

Traditionally, the span of a lifetime has been divided into a variety of sequential time periods. For example, in Shakespeare's play *As You Like It*, Jacques declares, "All the world's a stage, and all the men and women are merely players." After describing six discrete stages within a lifetime, Jacques concludes, "the last scene of all ends with second childishness and mere oblivion, sans teeth, sans eyes, sans taste, sans everything."

Within the human life span, sequential periods of time may traditionally be identified as "childhood," "adolescence," "adulthood," and "old age." Psychology professor G. Stanley Hall (1922) invented the term "senescence" to identify the years of later life. Hall held that society is on the point of crisis because of the forthcoming demographic certainty that persons will live longer and retire earlier than their forebears. Hall claimed that the result of this newly anticipated longevity will cause society to suffer from "boredom and unproductivity." As early as 1922, Hall rejected the so-called Scriptural life span of "three-score and ten years" and prophetically proclaimed that society should enable mature persons to plan at least twenty more years of meaningful involvement (Cole, 1992).

In view of the extended longevity we are currently experiencing, many older persons may be seriously concerned about the meaningful and satisfying use of so-called "free time" or "leisure time." In Moody's book, *The Abundance of Life* (1988), the author laments the voids and discontent that can be inherent in "the abundance of time" for many older adults. Moody suggests that to engage in life more meaningfully, we abandon the "linear life plan," which assigns specific tasks to fixed time periods, such as education and training in youth; work and employment in the middle years; and undefined "leisure and comfort" in later life. Moody endorses the "cyclical life plan," which involves reduced schooling and training during youth, more flexible retirement plans, and more options for education, work, employment, and leisure throughout one's adult life. In other words, Moody's advice is to "throw away the traditional clock," with its fixed time periods for specific tasks, and thereby enjoy a more flexible and rewarding life (Moody, 1988).

According to psychoanalyst Erik Erikson, the blueprint of human emotional development throughout life is summarized with the "Eight Stages of Man." Erikson suggests that life unfolds in eight stages of emotional growth, each one featuring a key emotional issue or developmental task that builds on each of the prior stages and establishes the foundation for continued emotional growth.

Erikson mapped out the psychosocial issues for infancy, early childhood, school age, adolescence, and young and mature adulthood. The key issues in the remaining two stages within a lifetime are the achievement of generativity over stagnation, and ego integrity over despair. Generativity involves a sense of care and concern for future generations rather than stagnation in the past. If we resolve all the earlier tasks of adulthood, and if we succeed in looking outside ourselves and caring for others through generativity, we may move to the final stage of ego integrity. This stage is aimed at establishing a sense of meaning in one's life, rather than having feelings of despair or bitterness that one's life has been wasted and unfulfilled.

Creativity and Aging

Accomplishments of persons in their later years are well known and usually earn public acclaim. Creativity, as a powerful inner resource, may find expression in the early decades of the twenties and thirties within one's lifetime. However, the ability to be creative and contribute to the culture may actually peak in the later years.

A book by Dr. G.D. Cohen, *The Creative Age* (2000), is filled with references to older persons who have been highly creative in their advanced years. For example, Michelangelo painted the striking frescoes in the Vatican chapel at the age of eighty-nine. Benjamin Franklin invented the bifocal lens when he was seventy-eight, and Frank Lloyd Wright completed the Guggenheim Museum when he was ninety-one. At the age of 104, a retired teacher, Sarah Delany, collaborated with her 102-year-old sister, Dr. Bessie Delany, a retired dentist, to write a book titled *Having Our Say: The Delany Sisters' First 100 Years*. This book became a *New York Times* bestseller and subsequently, a Broadway hit.

Dr. Cohen refers to the impressive accomplishments of older persons, which are highly lauded and applauded by the public, as exemplifying the "Big C" in Creativity. As a psychiatrist and geriatrician, Cohen maintains that while the "Big C" is applicable to the creativity of selected older persons who have gained well-deserved recognition, the "little c" in creativity is universally applicable to "all" older adults in their personal lives.

Cohen argues convincingly that every older person is capable of discovering his or her own creativity, be it a choice of a hobby, a new career, arts and crafts, new relationships, revitalized interests, a challenging new job, or involvement in volunteerism. Cohen's premise is that all older persons are endowed with the human urge for creativity. The experience of advanced years provides a unique combination of creativity and life events that promotes a dynamic dimension for inner growth.

Cohen refers to creativity as "an equal opportunity," which does not belong solely to the acclaimed artist's domain. He concedes that health complications are part of life for many older people, and that the risk of disabilities increases with age. However, he asserts that the creative spirit can find expression despite such obstacles. Cohen insists that the more mature years yearn for "something more" than the quantity of time. It is the desire for a "quality of time." As another writer on creativity says, instead of the lament of being "over the hill," the universal challenge for creative expression in life is the tantalizing prospect that "there is another peak to climb" (Czikszentmihalyi, 1996).

Aging and Time-Binding in the Twenty-First Century

With increased longevity, and the chance to be creative in advanced age, older persons have an opportunity to become more valuable time-binders, contributing to a richer and more advanced human culture. Society and individuals can help older persons take that opportunity by encouraging them to engage in creative pursuits and to interact more with younger people. Such efforts would be beneficial to all parties involved and, barring catastrophic events, make the twenty-first century the most notable so far in the history of human time-binding.

REFERENCES

Butler, R. N. (1969). "Age-Ism: Another form of bigotry." *The Gerontologist*, Vol. 9, No. 4, pp. 243-246.

Cohen, G. D. (2000). *The creative age: Awakening human potential in the second half of life*. NY: Harper Collins.

Cole, T. R. (1992). *The journey of life: A cultural history of aging in America*. Cambridge, MA: The Cambridge University Press.

Czikszentmihalyi, M. (1996). *Creativity: Flow and the psychology of discovery and invention*. Chapter 9, "Creative Aging." NY: Harper Collins.

Delaney, S. and B. Delaney (1996). *Having our say: The Delaney sisters' first 100 years*. New York, Dell.

Erikson, E. H. (1982). *The life cycle completed: A review*. NY: Norton.

Greenberg, S. (1990). *Words to live by: Selected writings of Rabbi S. Greenberg*. Northvale, NJ: Jason Aronson Inc.

Hooyman, N. & Kiyak, H. A. (1996). *Social gerontologist: A multidisciplinary perspective*. Nordham Heights, MA: Allyn and Bacon.

Kodish, S. P. & Kodish, B. I. (1993). *Drive yourself sane! Using the uncommon sense of general semantics*. Englewood, NJ: Institute of General Semantics.

Levinson, R. W. (2002). *New routes to human services: Information and referral*. NY: Springer.

Moody, H. R. (1988). *Abundance of life: Human development policies for an aging society*. NY: Columbia University Press.